This book is dedicated to my husband John M. Henry Jr., the love of my life, who seeks tirelessly to support me, who fell asleep at the bookstore on numerous occasions while he waited for me to finish writing; and to women that have ever wondered who they could call for a Word, a shoulder to cry on, a good laugh and a smile of affirmation anytime.

LOVE
BETTER LIVE
HAPPIER

A fun and simple guide to make and keep
godly friendships the way God designed
them to be; connected and joyful

No more messy girlfriendships

PASTOR GWEN HENRY

Quantum
Discovery
A LITERARY AGENCY

ISBN
978-1-959314-55-4 (Paperback)
978-1-959314-56-1 (eBook)
978-1-959314-54-7 (Hardcover)

TABLE OF CONTENTS

ACKNOWLEDGMENTS

There are so many people who helped me make this project come alive. First of all I acknowledge my Lord and Savior Jesus Christ who placed this ministry in my heart, this gift in my hands, and this destiny in my path. Nothing could be accomplished without Him. I give Him all praise and glory!

To my children: Jake, Kim, Chris, Ness, and Johnny who never assumed for a minute that I wouldn't write this book. The faith of children is awesome!

To my pastor-friend Elder Leonard Chapple Sr., who like Mordecai to Esther, allowed God to use him to help bring this destiny to pass.

To my church families, Latter Day Ministries COGIC, and Stronghold Christian Church who believed in me, cheered me on, and committed to buying my book. Actions do speak louder than words.

To my newest editor friend, Tracy Allen. You are a God send.

To Sherrell, my little sister in Christ and other ways, who strengthens me with her unconditional love.

To my sister-girlfriends, without whom the stories wouldn't get told.

FOCUS

Confess your faults one to another and pray for each other that ye may be healed; the effectual fervent prayer of a righteous (wo)man availeth much. James 5:16 King James Version (KJV)

FOREWORD

Communication is very important to our social and emotional well being. It allows us the opportunity to process information, seek wisdom and guidance, and just simply release our feelings. God often speaks of the benefits of us communicating with Him and with each other.

We all have secrets in our lives, things we want to talk about, but for obvious reasons we fear the reactions of the people we share our lives with. Then, there are times when you just want to vent. All you want is for someone to listen; and just say "uh uh," you don't want advice, nor criticism, but just for them to listen to you and nod every now and then so you know they are still listening.

Everyone needs a real friend who will tell them the truth no matter what the outcome. Someone who doesn't mind telling you when you are wrong, but also will go to bat for you when you are right.

We all need someone in our lives that we can be real with, no airs, who will still love us even after seeing us at our worst. Someone who will put up with us through our moods, (for women that can be a rollercoaster) cries with us, laughs with us, and supports us.

Love Better! Live Happier provides a means of allowing women to process their thoughts and feelings. It provides provoking conversation and self evaluation. It is just a good book to curl up with, relax and enjoy a good laugh. It's like talking to one of the sisters.

Dr. Sherry Gaither

INTRODUCTION

- *When we look at shows like Housewives of "anywhere" we see glamour, we see fun, but mostly we see drama. With episode titles like "Loose Lips and Lawsuits,- HWO Orange County and "Who's Calling Who a Fraud"- HWO Salt Lake City, and "I Would Never Say That."- HWO Beverly Hills it's not wonder women outside the limelight would prefer to stay shy of these "friendships." These shows "center around the connection the women have with each other. The deeper the friendships, the larger the drama, and the higher the ratings typically are." [1]*

- *The ratings may go up but these dramas and scrimmages result in many hurt feelings, broken friendships and even broken relationships that can lead to major trauma. They are the result of carnal living and carnal thinking. Messy.*

- *Fortunately, God's model of female friendships is not like this. God calls us to friendships that will inspire us, extend us, and encourage us. That's what this book is—a tool we can use to learn and confirm God's model of friendships among us ladies. We are not victims of the enemy's ploys to keep us apart. We are leading ladies in the friendship business if we allow God to design them. No more messy friendships.*

- *Do you know how many ladies leave conference after conference, workshops and even church services, only to eventually find themselves battling life's issues alone – without the loving prayers of a close sister?*

God made us that His love would flow freely from heart to heart but we seem to have a problem.

Jesus said in John 13: 35 *"By this shall all men know that we are His disciples by the love we have for each other."* People are not saying how much we love each other; they're saying how much we can't get along! We need a divine impact by God to stir things up and get His love poured out by the Holy Spirit moving again.

That's What this Book will Do for You

This book provides the tool and the opportunity to practice intentionally releasing and freeing the love that Christ has given you. The tool? Basic talk. 40 days of conversations, prayer and God's Word that will absolutely change the way you respond to your girlfriends, sisters, church-friends, and sister-friends- even for those not so friendly friends. Starting with those who are close to us or at least in close proximity is a great place to begin releasing the love of God. It is said that charity begins at home.

How Does it Work?

You and your friends will go on six planned fun times with good conversations within a 40-day span of time - 40 days of reading, thinking and focusing on sharing yourself in love with those who also love God. The Bible says in Proverbs 23:7 "For as he thinketh in his heart so is he:..." Proverbs 23:7a (King James Version).

Think of it as a trip. We love to take good, inspiring, fun trips, ladies. Doesn't everyone? Plan your six conversations like you would a trip where you will meet to discuss what insights, revelations and illuminations God has given you from your reading and meditation. Get your mind and your days ready.

You don't have to go at it alone; I have divided the book into four sections, a compilation of 40 short conversations in all. You can let your guards down because the format provides a comfortable atmosphere where my girlfriends and I open the conversations with our stories.

Every day you will read the day's entry and make notes about what you would like to share with your friends. When you get together on your planned outings, you share. That's it!

In your communication, you will discover a secret-something happening that may surprise you. A drawing together, a bonding, a sisterhood will develop. It's a proven fact that time spent together brings about connection. Now, don't allow the spirit of fear to rare it's ugly head. God hadn't us the spirit of fear but Power, Love and a Sound Mind. At the trip's end, you would have begun a wonderful, undeniable habit of releasing the love of God that fills hearts and wins souls. I've even given a list of ideas for places and activities you can choose from.

The Four Sections

The book is divided into four sections each with a different focus that will stimulate enlightening and encouraging conversations. Here they are:

Section I is called: Girlfriend to Girlfriend. It deals with some subjects that helps us to connect with each other and further understand the feminine roles in which God has destined us to walk.

Section II is called: Soul Connection. It deals with the best love of our lives, God, and reaches into our core identity which connects us to our source. It reminds us that we belong to the family of God.

Section III is called: Was it Good for You Too? It helps us to put our sexual and relational needs in God's perspective. Life can be great but sometimes life is not as good as we thought it would be. But with God's love freeing us we can accept His divine purpose and love others freely.

Section IV is called: Retreat. This part of the book provides a way for you and your girlfriends to retreat from the hustle and bustle of the day. It is the final lap, the last eight sessions that blanket us with the familiar comfort of emotional outlet releasing our souls to the loving Savior.

Other Features

Within the sections, except for **Retreat**, each chapter contains an *inspirational Poem/ Creative Prose* that quickly gets to the meat of the subject. (One of the quickest ways to a person's heart is through poetry.) This is followed by the *Author's Commentary,* intermittent with stories from my girlfriends. This is followed by a *Prayer* (reminding us that we are praying for each other together) and a *Scripture Verse or Verses* that lock in the principles discussed. (Our safety lies in the Word.)

The *Sister Tip* in each chapter is a practical and fun suggestion that helps you reach out to other women in building relationships and sharing Christ's love. Remember, "Faith without works is dead," (James 2:20). You can do these with your girlfriends who are taking the journey with you or others.

Discussion Starters will help get the talking between you and your girlfriends going strong.

Even though *Love Better! Live Happier* can be used as a personal devotional, or a ladies' bible study the entries were written to be discussed with your friends in social settings. I believe the experience with other hearts will add so much more insight.

> Special Tip: For best results, get your calendars out and see where you can begin your journey and safely complete it. Be on the lookout for distractions, hindrances and delays. The enemy of our souls hates relationships and will do everything to discourage you from starting and completing the journey. Beat him at his own game. When trouble comes to stop you, use your time together and pray against the tricks of the devil.
> Oh, and just in case you want to meet more than six times, feel free! The more you meet, the tighter the bond.

Meet My Girlfriends

I've decided to include the stories of my girlfriends as an example of sorts to the conversations you may have with your friends. It's a wonderful thing for me to share these friends with you because before I learned to love better, my friendship group was very small.

My new revelation: I can't live this life all alone and God doesn't want me to. I thank God for my girlfriends. Each one adds something to my life and gives me an opportunity to give back. It's like having a basket of beautiful flowers consistently around you. They're not perfect but neither am I. Our imperfections remind us that the ultimate friend is the one that sticks closer than a brother- Jesus.

Francine

When I met Francine she was sixteen years old on her wedding day! I remember being new in town and new to my church. I was sort of swept into attending the wedding. I didn't even know who were getting married but I was told that the whole church was invited.

Our real friendship didn't begin until my family and I became members of her dad's church. Music was our connector. She sang, I directed choirs, and our husbands were musicians. The constant communication between the couples brought our hearts together.

I was raised as an only child who always wanted sisters in my life. Because she was about ten years younger than me, Francine satisfied my longing by embracing me in the "big sister" role. I feel her trust and her love for me. I call her my little sister. We did a lot of growing together our friendship extended to both our entire families. God frequently puts her in my spirit when she needs a lift and I go running to find her. She in turn loves me unconditionally. I can't ask for more.

Heather

Heather was one of the sisters who attended the church I belonged to. I didn't really get to know her until several years later when the Lord impressed her to give one of her poems to me as an offering to this book. Her honesty is as straight as an arrow. She let me know she didn't really want to give me her poem but her love for God superseded her wants. So she gave it to me.

I had been looking for someone that shared my love for writing and my love for God with the spiritual maturity that would make our conversations intellectually and spiritually satisfying. Her personality was so different from mine that it never occurred to me that she would be the one and that we would become close friends. I had no clue she wrote too, but God strategically put us together.

She has become one of my "know it all" friends. When I call her for prayer or just to talk, she already has all my background information. It makes our time together so much simpler. We can get right to the issue at hand – and that girl can really pray.

Asia

Multiply my personality about three times and you'll have Asia's. She is full of energy and full of God. She started out as a student of our school. When she joined the church I attended, it gave us more time together. We struck up a friendship immediately because her intuition and playfulness intrigued me. Creatively and temperamentally, she was my match.

I remember one Sunday morning; we set out to perform an impromptu skit for the services that day. We only had about twenty minutes before the morning's worship service was to begin when we realized we needed a hat to make the scene complete. While some others wouldn't have dared to consider finding that hat on such short notice, we took the challenge and drove madly to the store about a half hour away to find it. For the whole trip we were rehearsing, writing the scene, crossing our fingers that we would make it in time, and laughing all the way there and back. Was it successful? Of course it was.

Asia is as strong as they come. She has been through a lot in her life but she refuses to allow the enemy of our souls to stop her. That kind of tenacity rubs off on a person.

Kim

Kim also took music lessons at our school. Every week I would see and speak to Kim. Casual conversations were as far as our acquaintance went. I wanted her to take part during the early stages of my ministry but she stayed aloof. So I didn't continue to pursue. Week by week we talked casually as we had always done especially when we stumbled on the subject of friendships – girlfriendships to be exact. It seemed that this was a sore spot for her and she had strong opinions about it. We saw eye to eye and shortly after, she began attending my *girlfriend to girlfriend* Bible study group.

She shared her stories of disillusionment concerning her girlfriends' commitment to the friendship. Together we brought the issues to God and received clarity on those issues through the Word.

Several weeks later she and my husband and I went out to a restaurant for a late lunch after classes. That's when our friendship blossomed; I'll never forget it. We ate and talked and ate some more and talked some more. They say the way to man's heart is through his stomach. I think it works for women, too. Deep connections were formed over food that day. We learned things about each other that gave us all a broader view. No wonder Jesus often ate with his disciples.

Kim is my "no nonsense, tell it like it is" friend. In love she'll tell you the truth. Everybody needs one of those in their life.

Renee

Renee is a great woman in ministry. She was a mentor and a good example to me. When I first became a member of my church, Renee was one of the leading ministers there. I was still struggling with my call to ministry then and was timid when I was asked to function in that office. She would playfully call me the "reluctant evangelist", pushing me to the front of things when I would try to hide behind the other ministers. She was the experienced one and I felt a sense of safety in her presence.

Our friendship blossomed when she invited my family and me to her house for dinner. Our families met and they made us feel like we had become an instant extension of theirs. I can't count the number of times we ate at Renee's house. Her husband is a great cook and loves to entertain. We'd eat, the children would play and the grown-ups would talk about almost anything.

Renee is a smart cookie. She always seems so confident in everything and when she makes mistakes, she doesn't have any problems laughing at herself. She is so cool and collected. Having a wonderful sense of fashion, her elegance doesn't exceed her generosity. I could "go shopping" in her closet whenever I needed that special something to make an ensemble work. I guess she's like a big sister.

Shannon

I met Shannon one day as she was coming out of the recording studio next to our music school. "Five foot no inches," is how she describes herself. She's a little bulldog when it comes to the anointing of God on her life. Shannon is also like my little sister in that she is younger than me, but when it comes to ministry she "ain't" no joke. I admire her ability to trust God for anything He leads her to do. She is a great woman of faith and she quickly became a friend to me. She was humble and easy to be around. With a fantastic singing and preaching voice, it's hard to imagine all of that power coming from such a small body. I think our friendship deepened when she decided to trust me with a very intimate testimony and prayer request. Of course I was honored to keep her confidence and I prayed fervently for her. Now, I'm sure I was not the only one praying for her but it's good to see the answers to prayer.

As a Pastor, her busy schedule doesn't allow for much girlfriend time but when we do see each other, it's as if we had not been away.

Joy

Joy is a friend whose demeanor gives me a place to put my funny remarks, and childish antics when I want to enjoy that part of my personality. She appreciates my humor and makes it easy for me to be myself. She is my "business-like friend." Her good-hearted nature is inviting; it puts me to ease. Joy is a pastor's wife. We met when her church and my church partnered together in ministry. But it wasn't until she became a student at our school that we were able to spend enough time together talking to really begin to know each other. I had the opportunity to pray for her during a difficult time in her life. Again, I was honored to have her share the details with me. Being approximately the same age gave us a platform for many discussions. We are so different in personality, style and interest that seeing us together would probably be striking to the naked eye. It is our hearts that are the same.

Early in our friendship, I remember feeling rather discouraged about the time it was taking to complete this book. So I called for support. I didn't know how to express what I was feeling at the time so I just rambled on and on. Patiently she listened and at the end she said in a matter of fact way with such calm finality that I should keep on working and that anything I did with faith in God will be successful. It was final and I felt like a child whose Mommy had solved an earth shattering problem with one kiss.

Barbara

Barbara was a later friend whose positive, bubbly personality won my heart quickly. Even though I've known Barbara professionally for some time, we were not really girlfriends, just acquaintances. She was a master of sales and I've always admired her ease in selling anything. She sold me right away when I contacted her professionally about ways to promote my ministry. I suspect she was just doing her job but something happened during our conversation that allured me to want to have closer communication with her. So after some prayer I asked her to serve on the board of directors for the ministry. She agreed.

It didn't take long to feel like we had known each other for an extended period of time. She had a way of enjoying life for what it presented and making it give the best it had to offer. She loves to entertain and will throw a party in a minute. Her heart is as big as Texas. On our first board induction ceremony for the ministry, she completely supported me. From the cooking, and serving food all the way to donating her beautiful house for the occasion, she was right on point. Maybe she'll teach me how to do the *Cha Cha Cha* one day.

Candace

Candace is my daughter-in-law and even though I knew her as a little girl, she has only been in my life for a short time. She's become the kind of friend that reminds me of myself years before. Her personality is very much like mine: 'artsy tartsy' and easy for me to understand. Because I am her mother-in-law, she also looks up to me as a mentor. She made it easy to share my wealth of experiences and watch them pay off in her life. Being a very creative young woman, she and my daughters would keep me abreast of the current fashions and styles. This is so important to me because it is an area that I don't know much about, (or is it that I don't seem to have the time to understand it?) Either way, she helps bring a fresh new outlook on many old themes. I need that as I get more seasoned in life.

JoAnne

I needed a prayer warrior to pray for my prayer line when I was just beginning the ministry and she came highly recommended. JoAnne dazzled me with her strong desire to pray for any and everything- anytime. Being a vibrant conversationalist, she gave me the opportunities to talk when the need arose.

Joanne and her New York accent made me feel close to home even though I now reside in Atlanta. We hit it off immediately. I felt so comfortable with her that on one of my birthdays I decided to spend it visiting JoAnne at her office, just her and I. Upon arrival I was so impressed with the set up.

That's when I discovered her anointing for shopping. JoAnne can find a bargain even when there is none in sight. She has a keen sense of spotting the perfect décor and can turn your mediocre function into a gala affair. Her heart is as big as her office was and when I left, my arms were full of gifts. I know when I need a warring prayer partner, JoAnne is always there. Every woman needs one of those.

* * *

I'm sharing my sisterhood with you through the pages of this book. Now it's your turn to share your sisterhood with your friends. But in case you are still not ready, read my story.

PART I

Understanding Why This Is So Important

CHAPTER 1

My Journey's Story

It wasn't until the morning I discovered a lump in my left breast, that I realized how important it was to cultivate deep connections to sisters and brothers in Christ.

The lump was about the size of a small egg. It was amazing to me, as if it had appeared one day without any warning. My immediate thought was the dreaded "C" word – Cancer. At that moment, my heart began to beat very fast, my stomach did an anxiety flip and my hands began to tremble and get sweaty. Almost suddenly, a fearful, long ago threat from Satan that I would die young and never see my dreams fulfilled became real to me. I looked up into my husband's questioning eyes and saw an expression of unbelief and helplessness on his face. I thought *not me, how could this happen to me?* But almost as soon as I realized my thoughts, the promise that God had given me many years ago shot up on the screens of my mind. The scripture Joel 2:25a captured my attention. It says, *"So I will restore to you the years that the swarming locust has eaten, The crawling locust, The consuming locust, And the chewing locust..."* That thought of the Lord giving me back my years, was like a raft I caught and held on to for dear hope. With it, the thought that the lump was only a cyst floated by and brought a calming effect to my heart. I said it to my husband; he confirmed that he was thinking the same thing. It answered the fear we were both feeling.

Unfortunately, a glitch in the hospital's system made me wait about a month to see the doctor. This circumstance gave time for two possibilities, one: a chance to increase my faith, and two: time for the enemy to attack my mind. Sickness and bad news have a way of bringing feelings of isolation. During the wait I remembered feeling extremely alone. I didn't want to upset my children until I knew there was a confirmed diagnosis, so I didn't tell them. Other family members included my sister and three brothers, but we had not grown up together. News to them needed to be delayed as well. I worked hard at managing the battle between fear and faith but I couldn't shake the feeling of isolation. Even though my husband was supportive, he was going through the ordeal as well. Anything that would suggest future plans compounded my sad feelings and sent me searching for more intimate support. I wanted women to walk with me through this process, who knew the power of God, who could identify with this particular trial and who would believe God for my deliverance.

I contacted a select few of my church girlfriends and told them what was happening. A month later when I finally got the chance to see the doctor I received a good report. The lump was indeed a cyst. Amen. Gladly, I called my "girlfriends" to share the relieving news. Only one remembered that I even had a doctor's appointment without reminding them. Well, I was hurt. It felt like they didn't care. *Were they real friends? I thought. What if the news had been devastating? Would they even be attentive?* I wondered if they had prayed for me or even thought about me. I know that life has many turns and responsibilities within the course of a week and my friends were busy ladies. Their forgetting of my doctor's appointment is understandable. Technically, I should have let my friends off the hook, but I was still hurt.

Even though I hadn't mentioned my hurt feelings to them, the enemy tried to take advantage of that opportunity to bring a wedge between us.

Loneliness embraced my heart like prison doors slamming. I tried to ignore my hurt feelings. I didn't bring those negative thoughts into captivity to the obedience of Christ like the Bible instructs in 1Corinthians 10:5. I didn't speak the Word, reminding myself that sometimes even though the spirits of my friends were willing; their everyday lives were filled with many responsibilities and concerns. Jesus experienced similar emotions in the garden of Gethsemane in Matthew 26: 40-43. No, I was hurt and all I could see was what I felt. My self-worth felt threatened and my sense of belonging felt disconnected. It is said that self preservation is the strongest human instinct; well, like second nature I built a castle. Rocks and bars on the outside, strong and full of contention on the inside.

The one friend that remembered my doctor's appointment kept hope for Christian sisterhood alive in me. She had made herself available throughout the whole episode. She called several times in the weeks to ask me how I was feeling. She invited me to spend time with her at her home while she went along her everyday family duties. Her sense of humor made me laugh and I could call on her to pray for me at anytime. I could share new events as they came up and didn't have to help her recall the particulars of my journey. It was very special to me because I knew the commitment she made. Her being a single mother with three children, holding a fulltime job, attending college, and working as a minister, didn't allow extra time to give. Her attention was intentional and she was diligent. Today we are not only sisters in Christ but true girlfriends.

> I began building emotional walls to protect my heart from future disappointments.

Changing my friendship quality

My friend taught me how to love intentionally. Her attention forced me to take a good hard look at the state of my other friendships. I discovered that I had not diligently attended to them. I took it for granted that we had an intimate relationship; *after all, weren't we sisters in Christ, with the character of Christ, "love your neighbor as yourself" and such like?* I thought to myself.

Almost there

The Bible says in Proverbs 18:24a says: If a man will have friends, he must first show himself friendly, (my paraphrase). I learned that what you sow you will reap (Psalms 126:5). I had to show the kind of deep friendship to others that I wanted to have given back to me.

If I wanted people to look out for me, check on me and care for me especially during troubled times, to remember me and my circumstances, I had to do the same thing. I had to attend to my sisterly relationships at the church.

Three quarters there

So that's what I did. I became intentional and diligent. I gave more attention to my sisters at the church. I did little things here and there: like text message them a little note wishing them a good day, or remembering something that I knew would be of interest and sharing that information with them. Little things don't take much time. When they needed a listening ear, I made myself available as much as I could to be there. Our relationships went to a level I hadn't imagined. The results proved true.

There

One day, I got a text message from a friend who had received a bad medical report and requested prayer. Well, immediately I prayed but also I forwarded the request to all of my girlfriends so they could pray too. I was so surprised when text after text, they responded ready to do holy battle against the enemy for my deliverance. I didn't realize that the forwarded message didn't include the original sender. My friends all thought it was me who had received the bad report. Even though it was mistaken identity, I was so blessed with the response, totally opposite from before.

CHAPTER 2

It's Hard to Take a Journey While You're Locked in a Castle

> Proverbs 18:19 "A brother offended is harder to be won over than a strong city, and [their] contentions separate them like the bars of a castle." (Amplified)

My story is not the only one of its kind. I've heard many stories that reflect disappointing expectations of intimate connections within our churches. I suspect many Christians have the same outlook and have become disillusioned when not treated as intimately as one may expect from the brothers and sisters in church. Most of us who have experienced this do survive and most continue attending church, but behind castle walls we've built to protect ourselves- the same kind of walls I began to build.

Consider the verse above. In Biblical days, the stone walls around a city were built to protect those who resided inside. A strong city is only as strong as its walls. Remember the city of Jericho? (Joshua 6). Its strength was the walls. God had to literally break down the walls to conquer the city for His glory. I know, sometimes walls are necessary to maintain a semblance of community. If it were not for those walls in some cases, there wouldn't be a sense of community at all. But that's the problem. It only appears to look like community. It's a semblance and the essence is thwarted and void of the relational satisfaction God intended for His people.

Rick Warren pens that in order to cultivate community it takes commitment, honesty, humility, courtesy, confidentiality and frequency.[2] Walls prevent the healing, the provision, and the goodness that God has placed within our connections from coming through.

Someone may say, *You don't know what So and So has done to me.* They're right, I don't know. Whatever it was, the offense affected them deeply. No argument here. But it is offense that separates good people from each other. It is the tool that the enemy uses to keep relationships from thriving.

The verse above refers to the strength and distance of the separation as castle bars. Castle bars are made of iron, one of the hardest metals around. It is almost impossible to move iron bars without breaking down the whole castle window and parts of the castle itself. So it is almost impossible to talk someone out of their offended soul. The issues are so strong it would take the power of God to break it down. Good news! God says He will take away the stony hearts and give us a heart of flesh- a new heart healed, delivered and set free, (Ezekiel 36:26). We have to be willing for the walls around our hearts to come down, hand our contentions over to Him and receive the healing love of God.

Our closed hearts affect God's heart

According to John 1:12, if you have accepted Jesus to come into your heart and have made him the Lord over your life, the Bible says that we are the children of God. There is little doubt that we love our father God. The love we have for our father God is often seen in the way we worship Him, and heard in our words, our songs and our expressions. As brothers and sisters however, it's not always seen in the way we relate to each other. Children are known to have scrimmages, but it breaks a parent's heart to witness their children arguing and distrusting each other.

As a parent I could relate. I remember how I felt at one of my birthday dinners. It had been a wonderful day for me. Everything I wanted to do that day I did. I met a special girlfriend and had a gourmet breakfast at McDonalds. I visited an art gallery and spoke to the artist there. I had a pedicure and ate lunch at a great vegetarian lunch spot. The climatic point of the celebration was to be dinner with the children at a wonderful seafood restaurant. Three of my children constantly argued with each other over the meal. Each was so engrossed in their point of view that they hadn't noticed how upset their arguing had made me. It was the lowest point for me in the whole celebration that year.

God's heart is broken when we do not demonstrate His love to each other. I agreed when people would say the worst place to tell anyone your business is in the church. I was one in the number to shout "Amen" when the word came forth reminding us to be careful about who we trusted in church, especially among the women. But soon after, something began happening to me every time those words would be spoken, especially when spoken from the pulpit. My heart would break; it was as devastating as if someone was talking about me personally. After months of feeling this pain, and God consistently bringing scriptures of love and unity to my spirit, I realized that God was showing me that it was His heart that was breaking. It was the same kind of hurt I felt when my children didn't seem to get along with each other. Jesus' commandment in John 13:35 says that the world would be able to identify His disciples by the love we have for each other (my paraphrase). In order for the world to make this identification, the love has to be noticeable. Our hearts have to be opened in order for His precious love to flow freely.

> God's heart is broken when we do not demonstrate His love to each other.

How do I open my heart?

Earlier we talked about breaking down the castle walls we built to protect our hearts from emotional injuries. Well, the first thing that has to happen in order to open your heart is to agree to allow others entry- to allow yourself to be known by others. Allow yourself to be authentic about your thoughts, and your feelings, about who you are inside.

The Bible not only refers to us as a family but also as the body of Christ. We're one body with members of different functions and whether we want to accept it or not, we're connected; it's difficult to live without each other. 1 Corinthians 12:21 "The eye cannot say to the hand, I don't need you."

Being Known is a Natural Desire

This is really not difficult because people have an innate desire to connect- to be known and to know others. If you think about it, it's the reason that social internet networks like *Facebook, and Myspace* are increasingly successful. High ratings from popular sitcoms like *Friends and even Seinfeld* attest to the fact that people enjoy watching friends interact in deep ways. It's natural.

Remember the theme song for the sitcom, *Cheers*? **"Sometimes you want to go - where everybody knows your name and they're always glad you came..."** [3]

Okay I admit it; I like to watch sitcoms. But it was God who started this whole desire to be known when He made us like Himself. He said to Jeremiah in Jeremiah 1:5, "Before I formed you in the womb I knew you; Before you were born I sanctified you; I ordained you a prophet to the nations." God wanted Jeremiah to know that He knew what was inside of him, what he was made of.

Jesus asked his disciples in Matthew 16:13-18, who others identified Him to be. They seemed to know exactly who people said He was. Jesus took it a step further. He wanted to know if His closest friends really knew who He was. When He asked them who they believed He was, only Peter spoke up and identified Him correctly. Jesus answered with Peter's correct identity as well and proclaimed that it was upon the rock of identity, He knowing us and we knowing Him, that He would build His church and the gates of hell will not prevail against it. Was it just about their names? It was much deeper than the name. Jewish custom dictated that names were not chosen by happenstance or nice sounds. "The name conveyed the nature and essence of the thing named. It represents the history and reputation of the one being named." [4]

When God changed Abram's name to Abraham it wasn't until after He had changed his destiny. His name reflected who God said he would be. It was a deeper identity. Everybody knew that Abraham was the father of many nations when they called him by his new name, (Genesis 17:5).

CHAPTER 3

It's Called Intimacy/ Who Really Cares About Me?

Webster's dictionary defines intimacy as, "a close, familiar, and usually affectionate or loving personal relationship with another person or group." [5]

In one of his messages, I heard T.D. Jakes, a famous televangelist, describe intimacy as "into- me- see", in other words, the opportunity and ability to see into each other, to be known. Don't be alarmed. Presenting yourself intimately to everyone is not advisable, practical, or probable but being open to love everyone is necessary to experience the close relationships that Christ tells us to have. Available to listen, to talk and pray for others, to spend time with others opens doors for close relationships to be formed. Intimacy answers the question: *who really cares about me?* Everybody needs to have an affirmative answer to that question.

Intimacy has different levels.

If it is not advisable to be open to everyone, how does intimacy work? There are different levels of intimacy. If you've noticed in Matthew 16, Jesus was speaking to His twelve disciples when He asked them to identify Him. There were many other followers of Christ; see Luke 10:17-20. These twelve were closer to Him. They had made a commitment to change their present situations to follow Him closely. Within the twelve Jesus had a closer level of intimacy still with Peter, James and John, (Matthew 17:9). In the gospels you can read where Jesus related to them a little more intimately than the others. You could call them His inner circle. These may have had special callings on their lives- a greater commitment or responsibility to the gospel of Christ, etc.

Callie Oliver and Erin Smalley in their book, *Grown Up Girlfriend*, Callie Oliver categorizes these different levels of intimacy into three categories she calls baskets. For instance, Basket Three is where she places the large group of acquaintances, Basket Two is for the smaller group with whom she would share herself occasionally, and Basket One is for those she calls the "know it all friends." These are the ones who are her closest friends.[6]

I like to relate my categories to the tabernacle design in the Old Testament, (Exodus 35): the Other Court friends being the largest group of acquaintances, Holy Place friends in the middle and the Holy of Holies, friends who are in my inner circle. It doesn't matter how they are categorized, just know that everyone does not belong on the same level.

How do you know how to categorize your friends?

Of course you are open to relate to everybody based on the amount of time you spend together, but when determining your inner circle help is needed. That's where the Holy Spirit comes in to lead us into all truth. Jesus told Peter that it was God who had revealed to him that Jesus wasn't just one of the prophets but the Anointed One, the son of God.

The first thing we have to do is rely on God the Holy Spirit, not our past experiences, to begin to know who God has placed in our lives for deep connection.

In another passage, John 10:27 Jesus says His sheep know His voice and will not follow a stranger. There is a "knowing" or identification in our spirit that calls to us deeply and confirms the voice of connection.

The second thing you have to do is bring your concerns for close friendships to God in prayer before you settle on who should be in your inner circle. Jesus prayed all night before choosing His disciples whom he would later call friends. See John 15: 14-15.

Intimacy Strengthens and Heals

Intimacy that is built on prayer and the Word of God easily supports an environment where supernatural strength in God and healing is available. The Bible tells us about the power of agreement in Matthew 18:19-20. He says that when two or more of us have come together in His name He is there with us (my paraphrase). If God is the center of your friendships, all of the benefits of the kingdom are in full force. Even though the gates of hell will try to attack the friendship, they will not prevail.

Supernatural Strength

In Judges 11 you can see the strength of intimacy in the daughter of a Jewish judge. The story tells us that this judge promised God that he would sacrifice the first thing that came out to greet him after a battle if God would give him victory. Jephthah was devastated when his only child, his daughter anxiously waiting to celebrate, came running out to greet him first. The Bible doesn't give her name, but for simplicity, let's call her Zoe. It was a rash vow Zoe's father had made to God but she knew he couldn't go back on his word. Zoe knew the God of her father and she knew the ramifications of her father's vow. Of course she was devastated.

What would you do with a death sentence looming over your head? That night Zoe made one request. Her last request wasn't to have a smoke, a drink, or even for a church service.

She requested to take her girlfriends with her into the mountains for two months to mourn her inevitable fate.

Now I could only suspect they cried together, prayed, reminisced about funny episodes or shared their anger about the whole thing. But whatever they did, Zoe must have known she could lean on her girlfriends for strength, love and empathy. What are girlfriends for? They could relate deeply and passionately to her plight as if it was happening to them. They understood what this tragedy specifically meant to her as opposed to just anybody- they knew her. There was no way that they would've allowed her to walk that journey by herself.

This rallying together would not have happened arbitrarily. It is my guess that Zoe and her girlfriends had cultivated and nourished a close, loving, personal relationship with each other beforehand. I think that this special request was easy for them to fulfill, giving Zoe strength to accept her fate.

The Bible also tells us that we are more powerful together in Deuteronomy 32:30, that one shall chase a thousand and two will put thousand to flight, my (paraphrase).

The Benefit of Healing

Connecting to each other in intimacy opens a path for tremendous power in our healings: physically, emotionally and spiritually.

Physical Healing

Medical science has proven the strong correlation between good health and having good friends. Not having good social relationships can harm your health the same way smoking 15 cigarettes a day or being an alcoholic can. Not being connected is found to be more harmful than not exercising, and twice as harmful on the body as obesity.[7]

"According to studies done, it was even found that people with strong friendships are less likely than others to get colds." [8]

"A 2006 study of nearly 3,000 nurses with breast cancer found that women without close friends were four times as likely to die from the disease as women with 10 or more friends. And notably, proximity and the amount of contact with a friend wasn't associated with survival. Just having friends, [intimate connections] was protective." [9]

Intimacy also boosts our physical healing through the Word of God. The Bible promises healing to those with faith to receive it. Faith comes by hearing the Word. Fear comes by hearing too, and the enemy of our souls often uses this tactic to terrorize us with thoughts of impeding danger associated with sickness. Battling bad thoughts will take a toll on our energy levels to believe God's Word. God can use our friends to bring the Word around us when we are too weak to get it for ourselves.

I remembered having strange pains in my stomach area and I wasn't sure what my ailments were. Of course the worst case scenarios consistently came to mind. I battled those thoughts, replacing them with the Word of God for healing. I put up a fight, but one night I was so exhausted it felt like the enemy was winning. I was so close to giving up and falling into a big pit of fear. I called one of my prayer warrior girlfriends. Because of our intimate friendship she already knew what I was dealing with. She began to encourage my heart with God's Words, reminding me about His promises to me and then she prayed. She prayed a prayer of faith and power that knocked the weight of Satan right out of my thoughts! I experienced a release of strength and I was able to continue fighting for my deliverance.

Emotional Healing

The Bible says in Romans 10:9,10 that believing and confession are what we do to be saved. It is good for our souls(that is our minds, wills, and emotions). We are one family in God and it's been known for family members to get on each others nerves at times. But when we allow hurts, bitterness and un-forgiveness to lurk in our hearts unchecked, we also allow the enemy access into our lives. Depressions, loneliness, stress, wrong beliefs, are items on a roadmap he has planned for our greater destruction. These soul aliments can draw us away into solitary living. Even though we may continue to physically assemble with people, we can close off our souls (mind, will, emotions) from others around us. That's exactly where Satan wants us to be- alone.

Luke 8:29 tells us that it was an evil spirit that influenced a possessed man to go into isolation. Being alone consistently for long periods of time has been documented to be detrimental to our perceptions.[10] Satan wants us alone to speak untruths to our hearts. These lies are sometimes believable if we have experienced hurt in our emotions. Before we know, we can find ourselves agreeing with the lies, without anyone available to see things through God's perspective. Intimacy opens the doors to honest communication. Our sisters in Christ can prevent us from spiraling down an ugly trail towards loneliness.

Spiritual Healing

Intimacy with others makes way for our spiritual healing to occur. I can't tell you the number of occasions that my girlfriends have inspired me to seek God for areas in my life that needed attention. Just through casual conversations I was able to see places where I needed to ask for help, even for forgiveness.

Intimacy in friendship can make it possible for those friends to help expose secret pain and can encourage us to release it to God.

Intimacy among our friendships gives opportunity to show humility, to accept being wrong as well as being right without having the right of way in our situations.

Intimacy within our churches and in our friendships give us opportunity to walk out the principles of the Word, to show the kind of unconditional love written in 1Corintians 13. Colossians 3: 14 tell us to forebear each other- to allow ease and forgive when there is a quarrel between us. God tells us to put on mercy, humility, patience, meekness, kindness. These attributes are not for the faint of heart; it takes the grace of God to love like this and to stay in close relationships in order to experience growth.

I love when God tells us in Matthew 5:23- 24 that if you are bringing worship to the Lord and remember that your brother has an offense against you go to him and make it right first before coming to God. Make room for forgiveness, ask for prayer if necessary. It's not that God doesn't want to hear from us, He is saving our lives.

Proverbs 14:30 says "A sound heart is the life of the flesh: but envy the rottenness of the bones."

The Fearful Side of Intimacy

Being known uncovers our strengths but it also exposes our weaknesses. We all have weaknesses and these are places of vulnerability. The last time I looked, vulnerability was not high on the credits list. It's understandable that we don't want to show our weaknesses. The world has encouraged us to hide them.

In the seventies, the lyrics of an advertisements jingle for a popular cologne were, *"I can bring home the bacon, fry it up in a pan and never let him forget he's a man,"* [11] suggesting the never ending strength of a working woman. Do you remember, the adage, "never let them see you sweat"? [12]

The scripture in James 5:16 and focal point for this book says the opposite. It tells us to: "Confess to one another therefore your faults (your slips, your false steps, your offenses, your sins) and pray [also] for one another, that you may be healed and restored [to a spiritual tone of mind and heart]. The earnest (heartfelt, continued) prayer of a righteous man makes tremendous power available [dynamic in its working]" (Amplified Version)

This verse doesn't instruct us to blab out our faults from center stage but it does suggest coming together with those who are righteous. Let's face it, most people would prefer to be seen in a good light, so most

> **"Why am I lonely in a crowded church?"**

of us stay incognito covering our true selves at church with the general "praise the Lord and blessed and highly favored" tagged to our greetings.

Wearing masks of painted on smiles and holy countenances have become an art form of sorts, when all along we could be having the worst time of our lives. We have gotten in the habit of protecting ourselves. This helps to create an environment of aloneness and loneliness that leaves women asking, "Why am I lonely in a crowded church?"

I know I touched on loneliness earlier in the discourse concerning emotional healing but I'd like to spend a little more time on it here. There is a difference between being alone and being lonely. "Aloneness is when you are socially isolated. Loneliness is when you are emotionally isolated."[13] Loneliness is a disease of the heart and it can lead to depression, suicidal thoughts and mal physical conditions. It doesn't matter how strong you are in your faith, loneliness goes directly against God's promise for our lives. Even though Elijah was a mighty prophet who commanded no rain for three years, he asked God to take his life when he became isolated from believers like himself. Most of the time, confessing fault, slips offenses and sins to each other requires a close, intimate, relationship with people whom you feel comfortable being yourself.

> **Through him we live, breathe and have our being. Through Him we can have our resurrection.**

Paul said in Philippians 3:10a, "That I may know him, and the power of his resurrection, AND the fellowship of his suffering (emphasis). We all would love to focus only on our successes, our good parts our "resurrections" but all of us have areas of vulnerabilities.

There is a bit of risk-taking in order to show our true selves. While deep connections can be heartwarming they could also be heartbreaking. God uses both as He works out His good pleasure within us. We are different with different experiences and different issues. But we all live in a fallen world and we have suffered brokenness, compliments of our forefather and foremother, Adam and Eve. We all need to be healed in some way and that's why we collide with each other on occasion. For some of us that brokenness is buried deep and requires a resurrection. Isn't it good to recognize that we can know Jesus in the power of His resurrection? "Through him we live, breathe and have our being." See Acts 17:28. Through Him we can have our resurrection. Truth be known, it is sometimes our friendship collisions that drives us to our knees in search of God- just where He wants us to be.

It Takes Faith in the Comforter

It seems like God always asks us to put ourselves at risk when we trust Him. It takes faith in God and our willingness to allow Him to protect us from emotional injuries. Without faith, it is still impossible to please God- even in this area.

Many have had their feelings stepped on, their business exposed and their reputation scarred as a result of confessing their faults. Hebrews 11, considered the faith chapter, tells us in verses 35-37 some of the atrocities the saints had to endure for the Gospel's sake. While the persecution was more of a physical nature, emotional suffering is just as costly. The faith of these forerunners, however, was heralded because of their love for God. It is an uncomfortable place to be but the rewards of trusting God for our personal emotional health are more than we could bargain for. The Holy Spirit is our comforter and He will always be with us even when we walk in the very valley of the shadow of death.

I have a dear friend who was molested as a child. He had never told anyone. It wasn't until after many years in his marriage he got the courage to tell his wife. We may wonder why it had taken him so long to divulge this experience even to his wife. A marriage relationship doesn't necessarily make it any safer or easier to unveil secrets. But this wife, being deeply connected to him, listened to him, empathized with him and prayed passionately for him.

Generally, he liked eating scrambled egg sandwiches but he would get nauseated eating eggs if they were on soft bread. He never knew why, it just happened.

One day out of the blue it seemed, the memory of the abuse came clear. He remembered that after he had been abused his molester had made an egg sandwich on soft bread and offered it to him. He had buried the incident so deeply within his mind that he couldn't remember the details. It didn't affect him then but those long ago details affected his present life.

When he was able to confess it, with prayer and love from his wife, deliverance came to him. The release gave him freedom from the pain, the blame, and shame. Now eating an egg sandwich on soft bread is not a problem. God had resurrected that part of him after being bound for over thirty years. God had the right timing and used the right person who was intimately connected to him for the occasion.

CHAPTER 4

Loving Yourself

If we don't release the Love of God for anyone else, we need to release it for ourselves. In John 5:1-13, the story is told of five covered walkways by a pool called Bathzatha where many sick people congregated. Among them was a man who had sat waiting to be healed year after year for thirty-eight years. Jesus came by and asked the man if he wanted to be healed. According to the man he was unable to get his healing when the waters were stirred because someone else would beat him to it.

It probably was comfortable to hang out with all of the sick people on Solomon's porch. I imagine they compared their wounds and aches and encouraged each other in their sicknesses, collaborating on the excuses for their inabilities to do many things. It was an intimacy of sorts, but one that was not founded on the Word of God but on sickness and self pity. Even though healing was being provided, this man couldn't seem to do what it took to get it.

It seemed a little callous to me when Jesus asked the lame man if he wanted to be made whole. After all, he was sick and appeared like he would want to be healed. What a strange question to ask someone in his condition.

The man never did answer the question but gave reasons why he didn't get to the water. But Jesus, saw through the justifications and called out his self pity. He asked him did he want to be made whole.

In order to release ourselves we have to want the healing enough to do whatever the Word of God instructs. Begin by releasing the offenses and the offenders in our lives, present and past.

Release the Offenses

The same question Jesus asked the lame man is the same question I ask now. Do you want to be whole? As long as we agree to live with disappointment, hurt, anger, and self pity in our hearts we are not whole. Some of us have lived wounded so long we've made ourselves comfortable with those wounds becoming a part of us, and justified our negative behaviors because of that fact. We might even find a community of others who have suffered just like we have and attach ourselves to them as the lame man did in the Bible.

Nursing these injuries gives a certain painful satisfaction to the flesh. We are blinded by our own rationalizations. So, we hold on to the offenses as if they were a safety net in our Christian walk that will protect us from further injuries. Even though healing is available, fear says *"don't go there- you're not familiar with it- suppose it doesn't work and you'll be hurt all over again."* So we prolong our healings with a false sense of security and decide not to reach for it.

But God has already sent us the Comforter. His name is the Holy Spirit. It is His job to provide our comfort, show us things to come and lead us into all truth, not ours. And all He asks us to do is take up our beds, our present circumstances, our issues, decide to be delivered and walk, towards healing. When we quench the Spirit of God from doing His job, we grieve Him and do a great disservice to ourselves.

Allow the Holy Spirit intimate access into your life, give Him your wounds. I promise He will revive you and you will be made whole. Isaiah 61: 3 tells us that Jesus came to trade out our heaviness, rejection, broken heart, torn spirit, inner hurt, and mourning for a garment of praise, our ashes for beauty and our heaviness for gladness. God knew we would endure these issues and He has already provided healing for them. Even though the odds are stacked in our favor, we can only be whole if we want to be whole.

Release the Offender

Not only do we release the offences to God but we have to release the offender to God as well. We cannot talk about wholeness without talking about forgiveness. People often said that hurting people hurt people.

It's difficult to understand the motives behind people's actions. But the Bible says in Ephesians 6:2 that *"we wrestle not against flesh and blood but against principalities, powers and the darkness of this world."* (KJV). Life is sometimes referred to as a war and we do wrestle with circumstances, situations, issues and even our own thoughts. If we haven't allowed God to fight our battles, our attempts to fix things ourselves can cause others to get injured. There are always causalities in a war where innocent people are hurt and killed. We are not to judge but to pray for those responsible, love them, to forgive them, to turn the other cheek. Turn the other cheek? Yes, you've read it right.

Turning the other cheek is a metaphor for forgiveness. Our natural inclination is to fight back or protect ourselves from the offense reoccurring. In turning the other cheek, God is saying for those situations, forgive and release to Him the natural inclination to protect ourselves. We want

> **"Fool me once shame on you, fool me twice shame on me."**

His protection not our own. In other words we are to forgive as if it never happened. Of course we're not talking about making the same mistakes, doing the same silly things, or putting ourselves in harm's way but in our hearts, forgive as if it never happened. An old friend of mine use to say, "fool me once shame on you, fool me twice shame on me." When we turn the other cheek, we're not being fooled; we are intentionally, shifting the responsibility for protection to God as we obey His commandment to love.

Doing this releases the offender from your revenge (no matter how subtle) and releases you from the torment of the offense. The enemy doesn't play fair.

When he encourages you to replay the offending incident over and over in your thoughts, it is a ploy to defeat you.

Along with the offense, he comes to bring suggestions of how awful the offense was, the intent of the offense, the implications of the offense (what it says about you) and the fear of it happening again with others. Those thoughts takes you to a place where your natural self esteem begins to suffer, your beliefs about yourself begin to suffer. It can create a negative reality where you're always expecting negative things to happen and you may begin to accommodate those negatives, even make explanations for them.

That environment sounds a lot like Lo-Debar (Lodebar). Lo-Debar was a real place during the reign of King Saul and then of King David, a city we read about in the Bible, (2Samuel 4:4; 2Samuel 9:4) whose name means *a place of no bread.*–where King Saul's grandson, Mephibosheth lived.[14] Even though he was in King Saul's family line, as a child Mephibosheth was lamed due to the accidental actions of his caretaker. King David discovered him, living life grossly below his potential, hiding out in this dismal city.[15] That's how we become in our souls when we hold on to offenses- lame and unable to live free lives in God.

We become the hurt ones and maybe unintentionally become the ones that hurt people. That is not what God wants for his children. He doesn't want us to live in a Lo-Debar- like environment. According to Ephesians 2:6, we have seats reserved in heavenly places around the throne of God. We're royalty. Our environment is one of peace, joy and love. We have to release our offenders in order to experience the abundant lifestyle Jesus promised us.

Easy to do? No way! This is not a natural way of thinking. It takes the supernatural power of God. Good news! His power is readily available for us. What we have to do is decide to take up our beds and walk toward our deliverance. God will do the rest.

CHAPTER 5

Women Have It

Dr. Gary Smalley, Christian author of family relationships, says in all of his travels doing conferences in 60 cities for 5 years he looked for but has never met a woman who by her God– given nature didn't possess a built in relationship manual.[1]

I believe it. I remember a time when I regularly rode the public transit system home from work, I took note that many conversational topics between women were about people and their interactions. Listening, I was able to piece together the scenarios that occurred even though I didn't know them or who they were talking about. The accounts were rich with descriptions from facial expressions, to voice inflections. Every detail as it pointed to the relationship of those involved was included.

Another time I spent a few days with my husband alone. I usually do most of the talking, but this time he was very talkative. I didn't want to hinder his free flow so I followed his lead. We talked about the weather, directions, space, traffic, and science. There was no talk of relationships or anything that connected the person or people. By the third day I found myself wishing I could find a girl to talk to. I was seriously having girl talk withdrawals.

Now I'm not suggesting that my meager number of experiences will substantiate Dr. Smalley's statement. He is a seasoned minister of relationships and has written many books on the subject. But it seems as if he's right; God has given women a great gift of relationship. From the start, according to the Bible in Genesis 1-2, He created both Adam and Eve with specific directives. Adam was told to dress the garden and keep it. He did that until God said *"that it was not good for mankind to be alone."* Then He made Eve. So Eve walked into conditions that were set for companionship. She was especially designed for it. We take after her in that deep down inside most women seem to have a gauge that sends a knowing of sorts to our consciousness when relationships are done right and an alert when they are done wrong.

Studies show that different from our male counterparts women thrive better when we have intimate, sisterly connections. This can be seen well during times of stress. Studies show in times of stress males respond with an behavior behavioral specialists called "fight or flight" women respond with "tend and befriend." In other words, women will experience a sense of comfort from stress by seeking out the companionship of other women for deep communication or by tending to children and/ or older people.[16]

> Friendship done right brings fulfillment.

After God began to tell me how to write this book, He said He wanted to *"unleash the power of His love among His children."* I understood better why this ministry is for women.

"Women are more concerned about people than projects; personalize their environment; speak with the language of the heart not the head; relate on multiple levels."[17] It's not unusual to see women eating, talking, laughing, or crying together. We need to be in each other's lives.

"We need a place to share our deep stories and expand our awareness through the stories of others."[18] When it's done right we are that much more fulfilled.

At the start of this book, I shared with you relationships done right. I could go on and on drawing the beautiful picture of friendships done right according to God's plan but it's time for you to get started releasing the flow of love that lives in your heart.

Now it's your turn.

Are you ready to begin? Remember, always pray for direction before you start any new venture. Take time and hear from God. You may choose to wait a week or more. I know that the Lord will bring you close to women who will bless you during this journey. If you already know who you will invite on the journey, begin.

PART II

Preparing for Your Journey

CHAPTER 6

Getting Started

Make a List

- Do you have girlfriends of your own? Make a list of girlfriends in your life. Maybe they are sisters in your church you might want to get to know better.

- It could even be your own biological sister that you enjoy spending time with, or maybe you need to get closer to her.

- Do you know who you would call if you had an emotional crisis?

- Which one of your sister-friends would you be comfortable calling in the middle of the night for words of encouragement?

- Who could you call to help celebrate something very special in your life?

- Who knows you? Really.

Don't have girlfriends of your own yet?

This is a great opportunity for God to bless you with good friends. You will have to walk by faith and show yourself friendly.

- Pray and ask God to show you women who could use a friend. Then begin to look. Faith without works is dead.

- Look for sisters in the church about whom you enjoy anything, (eg. their company, their talent or gift, their style, their ministry, or even their smile).

- Do something small to make contact, (compliment them and let them know how they bless you or you can give a greeting card of encouragement).

- You may even want to come alongside and bless another sister who could use a good friend in Christ near her.

Survey Your Relationships.

You should now have a broad idea of your sister-girlfriend climate, and have identified the ladies you have or may want to have as friends or even close friends.

Keeping a prayerful attitude, choose who you will ask to journey with you, not more than four others, and not less than two others.

Formally invite them to take this journey along with you. You can Even print out special invitations online. However you invite them, make it a special occasion.

How does it Work?

The principle steps of taking this journey are **time, risk, opportunity** and **talk.** Taking these steps will begin to help bring the closeness of hearts into the group. **T.R.O.T.** It's a slow trot but worth every step.

By reading the entries each day, you are committing the <u>time.</u> The guidebook consists of 40 days of subjects for conversations that will minister and refresh your souls. Read one each day. In this way you can use it for a devotional.

By opening up your heart to the subject matter and preparing to share your thoughts, you are taking the <u>risk</u>. Each of you will daily read the day's entry on your own time, noting points and thoughts of one or two interest that you will want to share. It is freeing and humbling to be honest with your thoughts and feelings. The bonding happens when others can hear their stories through yours.

By agreeing to meet with your group on six special dates, you are taking the <u>opportunity</u> available to you. Make arrangements to meet together for special conversations six times. Phone conference calls, girls' night out, even weekend retreats, Zoom or facetime, having lunch together or hanging out at each other's homes could be ways to meet.

By sharing your thoughts you are talking together. Talk is that special ingredient that opens the doors to our hearts. Use the *Discussion Starters* in each entry to help get the conversation going and extend your talk to the bonding truth of God's Word.

RETREAT

The last section of the book is called Retreat. This section is designed to offer a resemblance of getting away. Music and snack suggestions are offered to help you create an ambience. Of course you can create your own as well. We seal this experience by giving you an opportunity to write your own prayers to God, awaiting His answer. We know He hears and answers our prayers even when we have to vent. This part may remain just between you and God or it can be shared, you be the judge. You can actually plan to go on a retreat with your friends.

PART III

The Trip

GIRLFRIEND TO GIRLFRIEND

Welcome to the first section of the journey. As you enter this section, you will experience the familiar talk of girlfriends talking to girlfriends.

For some of you this is a big step of faith. Remember that our faith lies in the Almighty God - the creator of relationships. You are in good hands.

No doubt the journey will take you on some straight and curvy roads, but growth normally does.

Be ready to take notes because I'm sure there will be much to learn about yourself and your traveling buddies that will enhance your walk with God and with others.

Note: Don't forget to read the poems on the left to give you a quick overview of the subject. It may even minister to you.

Words of Inspiration:

When God made woman
He must've stood back and
admired her
and if God wasn't God,
He would have marveled
watching her stretch towards
heaven welcoming her
creation poised like a
dandelion after a spring rain

His mouth would've
dropped open at how
the light in her eyes
illuminated His glory
reflecting it in every direction
brightening the corners of the earth

He would've been awestruck
at the sound of her voice that
warmed the atmosphere like the
sounds of summer lips forming
words shaped in comfort

not to mention the details that
chose her attention He wouldn't
have been able to stand it as she
strutted along side Him in the
cool of the day, perusing and
choosing the beauty of her
surroundings and the delicate
touch of her hands reaching
out to heal, comfort and restore
would've sent His mind spinning

trying to understand that
kind of caring... If God
wasn't God amazement
would've overwhelmed
Him when He
witnessed her agility
and her ability to
ride out the storm, standing defiant
like a palm tree that never breaks

But God is God and worthy to be
praised He wasn't surprised; He
made us in His likeness Formed
us in His image Beautiful, before
the foundation of the world ..and
He meant to do it!

You Are So Beautiful

Every woman wants to be beautiful- "the crescendo, the final astonishing work of God."[19] We want the important men in our lives to desire us and other people to enjoy our company. God made women in His likeness and image; and like God we want those in our environment to experience our glory.

Matthew 13:22 says the cares of life will choke the Word out of us (my paraphrase). When we get bogged down with living, going to work, working at church, being a wife and mother, etc., it's easy to put ourselves last or forget ourselves altogether.

Eventually we feel as country singer Randy Travis describes in his song, like an old pair of shoes.[20]

Girlfriend Talk

(Gwen) *"Years ago our family was asked to appear in a special CBS news report on "The High Cost of Raising Children." The news team followed me as I went about my hectic schedule. I had it down to a science: working at a daycare center until five p.m., picking up our five children from another daycare and after school center by six p.m., going home, preparing and sitting down to dinner. The news team even followed me to rehearsal. Yes, on top of everything else I also sang in my husband's band in addition to directing the church choir and being a full time student. I was doing far too much. There was no time to pay attention to me. It wasn't until years later while watching the video again that I noticed I hadn't even taken the time to spruce myself up a bit before the interview. I still wore that tired big "no fuss" wig I had resigned myself to wearing back then, no make-up or jewelry. I was a "make do" woman getting the job done just like my granny taught me. The worst thing about it was that it took me several years to realize it. Since then my daughters have taught me the joys of taking time for my own personal beauty. Thank God!"*

* * *

Whatever your sense of beauty may be, display it. I hope you don't feel like an old pair of shoes because you're a work of art. Beauty is not only pleasant to look at but it is powerful. "It is the essence of God's glory."[21] Like a baby's soft skin stimulates life-giving cuddles from its family members, so our beauty encourages others to satisfy our need for healthy attention. Of course sometimes our beauty encourages the wrong attention, but that's due to sin in the world. Don't allow anyone to degrade you, abuse you or manipulate you into being less than you were created to be. God expects us to experience, look upon and enjoy our beauty. It is an occasion to praise God. When it's all said and done, make sure your beauty is not only skin deep. Adorn your insides with the spirit of meekness in the beauty of holiness.

SISTER TIP: Throw a praise party to celebrate your womanhood. Invite someone who could use a lift. Reach out to her. Too long we've cried together. This sounds like a celebration event. Let's laugh together. God is still good.

Pray Together:

God, Thank You for making us women in the image and likeness of Your beauty. What an honor to serve You from this place. Help us to walk in the royalty that You intended us to walk in, to give respect to Your creation by praising you in our bodies. We want to honor You with our hearts and celebrate You through our lives. For our sisters who have been abused and misused, we pray for a deep healing that will change the bitter waters of Mara to living waters springing into everlasting life. Help us who come in their presence to bring a spirit of peace, joy and longsuffering. In Jesus' name we pray, Amen.

READ THIS:

"I will praise thee; for I am fearfully and wonderfully made: marvelous are thy works: and that my soul knoweth right well." Psalms 139:14 (KJV)

DISCUSSION STARTERS:

- If you could enter any part of your body into a pageant, what part would it be and why?

- Describe a time you felt really beautiful.

- Describe a time you didn't feel beautiful.

Notes:

Words of Inspiration:

We stand together
united as a powerful force
rising to the cause of Christ

Through man made laws
depression, sexism, oppression,
and just being taken advantage of

We make it thickening the cords

Through, mood swings and
monthly
cramps and in the face of fear

Through being ignored,
overworked and over looked

Birds of a feather directed in
divine
flight perched in beautiful
boldness

Gaining strength from generation
to
generation taking our place in
formation
Standing!

Along side Queen Esther Faithful!
looked death in the face, save a
nation

Beside Mary confident in God's
promises

opened her virgin womb brought
forth the
Savior of the world

Next to Rahab visionary of
righteousness
Used herself as a diversion for the
army of God

Close by Deborah
rose above the odds judged a
promised people

Connected with Ruth
Humble obedient positioned
in the blessed line of the Messiah

Partners with Mary Magdalene
Desired God
ignore her soiled past,
crossed binding customs
Reached the Savior

We're sisters of the same cloth
daring, dazzling
marching through the ages
Grandmothers, mothers and
daughters strength to
strength with one voice

In the Company of Sisters

I DON'T CARE HOW IT FEELS, YOU ARE NOT ALONE! From creation, women have gone through the same experiences that you undergo today. I |am| so glad God wired our emotional system to bond with other women. We need to connect especially during times of stress. Being a woman in a man's world can be difficult. Sometimes even the Word of God is misconstrued bringing undue burdens on women. Responsibilities in life can drain us until we have nothing left. We need our sisters for support.

I remember trying to explain how absolutely worn out I was after holding, working, and caring for three small children through two, sometimes three services at church on Sunday while my husband performed his duties as a musician. He was sympathetic but I could see from his eyes he didn't really "get it."

When my emotions run like a roller coaster, up and down and all around, I need to talk to someone who can relate, who's been there and made it through. I need someone who doesn't need words to feel the depth of my concerns. I call on my sisters in the gospel, the Paula Whites, the Joyce Meyers, the Taffi Dollars of my day. They have made a commitment to serving God. I know they have experienced what I am going through and have come out shining in victory. Just watching them minister the Word of God gives me a push to keep going.

Girlfriend Talk

(Gwen) *"I felt very comfortable talking to Kim about something that has kept me going around in circles for years. It always seemed so intricate and difficult to explain to others. I'd shy away from sharing despite my desperate need to get clarity. Kim made herself available for the talking. We didn't plan any particular course of conversation, but the subject presented itself and I followed it through. Even though she is several years younger, I trusted her devotion and love for God. I knew she would be a conduit of his wisdom and love to me. Not only did she listen attentively, for as long as it took, she asked questions that helped me unpack the emotions and wrong beliefs about the issue. I didn't expect Kim to solve my issue, but her company as I walked through the hurt gave me courage to continue walking until I reached the truth."*

* * *

Whom do you call to keep good company with? You can tell a lot about a person by the company they keep. Is it someone who will remind you of the promises of God, who will help carry your burdens to the Lord? I call them my "fallout" sisters because I can allow my issues to fall out of me right in front of them.

It may be women in your church or even a television evangelist who can help you. Listening to their sermons and reading their books will reveal many personal experiences that may mirror some of yours.

I find company also in the stories from the women in the Bible. Our environments, mechanics or expressions maybe different, but our emotions, our needs and our desires are the same. Let the Lord minister to you through their stories.

SISTER TIP: *Today, if you need a little lift, call one of your "fallout" sisters and have a cup of tea, or better yet, go shopping. Two or three of you praying together creates a bond between women like none other. This may take a little planning but it's worth the effort.*

Pray Together:

Thank you, Lord for putting examples of victory through Your Word, through our church family and friends and even through the media. Help us to stay close to each other in Godly love. We bind up discord, misunderstandings and fear out of our bonding. We know that we're stronger together and that your perfect love will banish all negative things. In Jesus' name we pray, Amen.

READ THIS:

"Bear one another's burdens and so fulfill the law of Christ." Galatians 6:2 (NKJV)

DISCUSSION STARTERS:

- Many women say they prefer men's company to that of women.

- Why do you think this is so?

- What is your position and why?

Notes:

Words of Inspiration:

My sister with her many insecurities
sometimes almost drowns me they
drape around my neck and weigh
me down like a bad check

I sense the scent of fear around
her before it appears and by the
words from her mouth close by the
other
spirits stake out

Oh no, not again, not today I pray
don't have the energy to say
encouraging words

am I my sister's keeper? am I
the one that God sent to expose
the enemy's bent?

in my sister's weak state her
feelings blue am I the one God's
sending the answer through?

God.
remind me of the time
my faith was on the blink

how you sent one of my
sisters to be my spiritual
interlink...

my sister who saw my faults
but called them weaknesses
who stood in the gap when
my spirit was zapped

she prayed a prayer for me
that only a sister in Christ
could relate to
I felt her spirit
groan for me I felt my
deliverance break through

we must hold each other up
with our special spirit of caring
anointed, discerning we know
what each of us is bearing

so are we our sister's keeper?
God give us the patience to
be strong links in a prayer
chain heard continuous
strength transferred

Am I My Sister's Keeper (for Marjorie)

It's amazing what the prayers (the caring, non-judgmental intercession on someone's behalf) of a godly sister can do to lift someone else's spirit. Interceding is serious business. To intercede means to go in for another. Often times God impresses us to pray for a sister in crisis. We may or may not know her well and she may be too weak to pray for herself. It will take your prayers for a breakthrough to her victory. God has created women with a keen sense of intuition that, along with the anointing of His Spirit, picks up when others are hurting. Smack in the middle of a prayer, He has a way of putting a picture or thought of someone in your mind. Are you the one in need?

Girlfriend Talk

(Gwen) *"I remember one day after church, Francine noticed that I was upset (not having a good day would be a gross understatement.) She stopped and asked me how I was doing. Another time I might have brushed it off by saying something like 'just pray for me girl,' but that day I was at my wits end. I needed to 'spill my guts.' It was all I could do to keep from bawling.*

She didn't run away from my drama, and that was important. Instead, she embraced me with her listening heart and insight, I knew came from God.

I was grateful she made herself available to me. It didn't take a lot of time, but I felt my burden melt away as she briefly spoke with me. Sometimes all it takes to feel better is a listening ear."

* * *

Let God use you even when you don't feel like it. Your breakthrough may be wrapped up in hers. If we practice being sensitive to each other's needs the enemy of our salvation won't have many opportunities to defeat us. Intercession doesn't stop with prayer. Prayers have legs. Intercession may require us to do something as well.

> *SISTER TIP: Ask God to lead you to someone and allow the Holy Spirit to guide your mind to someone during your prayer time. Be led of the Lord! Minister to that sister. Talk to her, be her strength, bring hope, bring love.*

Pray Together:

Lord, thank You for giving sisters that can surround us with prayer and the Word of God. Help us to make connections and reach out to each other through Your Spirit of love. Encourage us not to run away but renew us as we intercede for each other. Help us to have patience with each other as we delve into each life. Make us one like you are with your father. In Jesus' name we pray, Amen.

READ THIS:

"Confess to one another therefore your faults (your slips, your false steps, your offenses, your sins) and pray (also) for one another, that you may be healed and restored (to a spiritual tone of mind and heart) the earnest (heartfelt, continued prayer of a righteous man makes tremendous power available (dynamic in its working)." James 5:16 (AMPLIFIED BIBLE)

DISCUSSION STARTERS:

- Describe a time when you were too tired to help another sister with her problems.

- Describe an experience when you did.

- Interceding can be physical, emotional as well as spiritual. Talk about the times you interceded for another sister in these ways.

Notes:

Words of Inspiration:

I see your smile bright as a 100-watt bulb
excitement like fireflies around your head
things going soooo goooood

dreams coming to past
God's blessing right up on the surface
clear as a just washed glass

frustration in another galaxy
patchwork covers on somebody
else's bed empty refrigerator,
bare cabinets just memories

depression skipped away like
a dog with its tail between its
legs, look where God has
brought you from

you're a prophecy fulfilled
you've been through the fire
and the smell of new leather
displaced the smell of smoke

you're in your rightful place
Drive girl!
in the splendor of the Master's
grace, drive into the joy that fills
our hearts, our sister has come
through great trials, now is the
time of the singing of birds

the morning arise and we
celebrate God in your victory

Mercedes Driving Sister (for Yvonne)

Have you ever met a woman that just kept on going no matter what life threw her? Doesn't watching her go through life like a locomotive makes you want to see her blessed?

Girlfriend Talk

(Gwen) *"An insurance agent once showed me a picture of the effects his Mercedes had suffered due to a car accident. He pointed out how even though the car was totaled, because of the iron frame around the driver's seat, he was spared. It was then that I decided that the Mercedes Benz was the kind of car I wanted to drive. It was beautiful, elegant and safe. When I think of my girlfriends, I think of them as not only being beautiful and durable but safe to be around. If blessings were cars, I would consider the Mercedes Benz to be a top notch blessing. My girlfriends deserve that."*

(Gwen) *"Asia has been through so much trouble in her Christian life. God has called her to an awesome ministry and the enemy has tried unsuccessfully to put her out of commission. From homelessness to cancer, you name it, she's been through it. When we first met, Asia had just been released from her job in the medical field. As a single parent, she was distraught. She had a talent for designing floral arrangements. I suggested she start her own business with her arrangements. Before her business took off, we both suffered together. I remember feeling the pain every time something crazy happened. I was angry at whoever hurt her and happy for all good things in her life."*

"Soon after, she not only did floral arrangements but her scope extended to doing weddings. I remembered she had so many weddings to do she was exhausted. But we were so excited. Many times when she had a profitable event, we'd go out and celebrate together. Now when you see her, you would never imagine that she had gone through anything. Her strength is amazing. Even though I know it is God's grace, I can't imagine myself enduring such trauma.

My respect for her tripled, and my trust in God grew deeper. God showed Himself mighty and strong through her."

* * *

Rejoicing with someone during her victory is a blessing that floats back to you. You were there during her tears, her fears and her distresses. Because you cried along, prayed along and suffered along with her, you're able to see how God brought her out. It strengthens your faith. The whole experience says, if God can do it for her, He can do it for you.

Jealousy has no place here even though it tries to rear its ugly head. It causes us to search for negative points in others that when compared to ourselves makes us superior in some way. Or sometimes we may find ourselves withdrawing from our friend because we feel left out, sad or even angry. Who needs that? A few potent words of scripture, faith and a decision to obey God will "nip that in the bud." Don't allow the enemy to put a damper on God's blessings. Join her in praise. Think about it. Has God opened some doors for a sister in Christ? Or is she in the suffering stage?

SISTER TIP: Rejoice with her through the good times or encourage her through the hard times. We don't have to walk this walk alone. No fun to eat alone either. Go out together and do that. Wonderful things happen around food. Yummy!

Pray Together:

Father, thank You for good friends and companionship. In Your Word, You tell us if we suffer with You we will reign with You. Help us to encourage each other during times of suffering and help us to remember You as we rejoice together.

Speak to our hearts as we strive not to be selfish or jealous of our sisters' blessings but bind us together in Your love as we show the world that we are your disciples. In Jesus' name we pray, Amen.

READ THIS:

"And now abide faith, hope, love, these three; but the greatest of these is love." 1 Corinthians 13:13 (KJV)

DISCUSSION STARTERS:

- Describe a time that you almost felt the pain of what your girlfriend was going through and what you did to alleviate it.

- Would you admit a time when you've felt jealous of your sister's blessing? Describe it.

Notes:

Words of Inspiration:

When women get together
to talk about Jesus
it's like sisters around the
kitchen table baking bread
rich, warm and close, talking
'bout Jesus, sifting down
worries, troubles and burdens
reducing the pinch of the
devils attacks bringing them
into divine perspective, mixing
up experiences cold and hot
marveling at how God worked
things out, kneading in the
promises of God past and
present leads us to still waters
restores our souls, resting under
a clean covering of the Word
makes faith rise like yeast
pushing out testimonies cutting
into pain shaping out blessings
reminding us that Jesus can still
change water into wine, receiving
God's love, we open our hearts like
a hot oven releasing a sweet smelling
savor of worship ooooh sooooo
comforting, tastes good to the
tongue too

Baking Bread

Talking has gotten a bad rap. Good talking brings women together like the smell of bread baking in the oven does for a family, it does them good. Uplifting, encouraging words is what we're talking about.

Because we rarely leave a conversation the same way we came into it, special care has to be taken. It's second nature for most of us to start or participate in a conversation, even if we're the one that actively listens. Remember it takes two to have a conversation, the talker and the listener.

The Bible says in Proverbs 18:20, that our words form our environments, (my paraphrase.) If we talk good talk then our environment will be good. We will be energized, encouraged, and renewed and enlightened. The environment is listening.

Girlfriend Talk

(Shannon) *"Being a Pastor keeps me busy that I sometimes get lost in my work. But when my mother bakes her sweet potato pies the aroma pulls me out into the kitchen. There, I would end up spending precious time with her. If it wasn't for those pies many times I would have missed some great bonding time with my Mom."*

(Shannon) "I was visiting a friend for dinner when I met a woman named Maxine who had recently been married. We sat in the kitchen talking, waiting for those good-smelling salmon croquettes. Maxine began to share her story about the time she almost married her best friend and how God led her in another direction, the one He had for her. She didn't know that I, being single, was dealing with the same issues. I had just broken up with my best friend- the man I knew I was gonna marry. As she shared her testimony I connected with her right away. She was telling my story. Hope and faith started to rise in my spirit. It took away the confusion and questions that were there. I wasn't crazy after all and I hadn't missed my opportunity. Whew!"

* * *

I can understand not engaging in negative talk like gossip and back biting, but that's no reason to cut your blessings off completely. When we're going through circumstances, life's burdens can outweigh what we know about God. It's easy to lose faith through our lives. That's when we need to remind each other about how wonderful, how capable, how powerful, how all knowing, how loving God is. The Lord lives in the praises of His people. Psalms 22:3 (my paraphrase.) God meets us in the talk. Ladies we know how to do it right. When the Lord is present, visions are born, destinies are realized, burdens are lifted, strong holds are revealed, and deliverance is received. So talk, girl.

> *SISTER TIP: Get with a girlfriend and "knock yourself out." Talk about how good God has been during all of your life cycles. Share your testimony. God has been good to you and your friends. You'll be surprised at how energized you'll feel.*

Pray Together:

Lord thank You for the ability to talk about Your goodness with sisters in the Lord; each one brings something to the table that blesses us. Help us not to use our precious gift of communication in anger, strife, or gossip. Let us find Your hope, insight and encouragement

in our sharing together. For those of us who have been hurt through talk, give us the grace to forgive and the courage to engage and receive from our sisters' wisdom, their strength, their experiences and their love. In Jesus' name, we pray, Amen.

READ THIS:

"I will meditate also of all thy work, and talk of all thy doings." Psalms 77:12 (KJV)

DISCUSSION STARTERS:

C.S. Lewis said, "Friendship is born the moment one says to another, 'What! You too? I thought I was the only one.'"[22]

- Describe a time when you've been in a conversation with other women and you were able to identify with someone's feelings or experiences.

- Tell about a time when you've gone to a ladies' group function and left with a friendship.

Notes:

Words of Inspiration:

You go girl!
with your ensemble,
you wearing that hat
and where did you find
that off shade
to match those shoes?
Like sea salt water on a cloudy day,
Interesting color.
Girl!
you got it goin' on
but where is the main
Accessory?
no, not the hat pin
even though that is sharp, making a
confident statement
are those diamond snake eyes
flashing
green,
subtle, moving?
Girl only you would've found
something
like that.
But I'm talking about the thing.
You know the thing
that brings it all together.
no, better than a broach or a feather.
you know that feature
that strikes out when you first
walk into a room.
no, not the make up
even though the make up is
beautiful as
usual

you know what I mean though
the cologne?
that's always been my favorite
fragrance
and you do wear it well.
but no, no not that
can't you tell?
come on you know
what piece is missing.
you know,
the hope, the joy, the peace, the
light,
the light in your eyes.

Dressed Up

Hello in there. Yeah, you!

I 'm talking to you with your sharp, intelligent, capable, well-dressed, well-educated, good looking, and controlled, detailed, religious, fun-loving self.

Yeah, we cover our true feelings and hide behind all kinds of masks. As we battle life, we put up a brave front. Sometimes we have to do what we have to do to survive. Being women, we know how to mask the rough stuff. Dressing up helps keep our emotions under wraps, especially when we don't have the privilege, the time, the strength or the will to deal with the issues at hand. It's a funny thing about masks; they never cover your eyes.

Girlfriend Talk

(Asia) *"I suspected my husband was being unfaithful. Things started to feel wrong and he acted funny. When you've been married to a man for ten years you can tell. It came out the night I was scheduled to preach at a church service. I couldn't deal with it then but as I got myself ready, I used every stroke of make-up and every well-placed curl like weapons of war. I emerged from my dressing room gorgeous on the outside, dying on the inside. What I saw in the mirror gave me a second hand feeling of acceptance in the middle of overwhelming rejection. It was very painful but finally I had to release my pain to the Lord for true deliverance to happen in my life."*

* * *

God knows your pain. He knows the origin, the circumstances, the complications, the nuances, and the solution. Maybe you've lived in a hurtful environment for so long, it's difficult to identify the initial problem anymore - but the pain is still real. Whether you were responsible for it or not doesn't change God's feelings about you. God still loves you and He gives grace for times like these. Being unfulfilled, stressed out and hiding is no way to live the abundant life Christ died to give us. Release yourself today. Go to God in prayer. Come clean with your feelings. Don't hold back anything. Don't you think its time for you to be delivered from this bondage?

You may think no one else can detect it, but burdens show in our walk, in our words, and mostly in our eyes. Trust God, things won't stay the same. "As you wait on God through your season of weeping, His promise to you is sure and you can expect Him to do as He has said."[23]

You don't have to keep the secrets any more.

SISTER TIP: Find a sister with whom you can pull down the guards and be "real." Then release the pain. Be available for others to come to you for help. You may need to pour your heart out to God for another sister in need. Afterwards, send this poem with a note saying you've prayed for her today.

Pray Together:

Lord, how great You are to tell us to throw our cares on You because You care for us. We come to do that, to give You our masks. We lift them up to You and we let them go. Take away the need to hide; cover us with Your love. Today we release our hurts, our stresses, our sad thinking, our tears, our faults, and ourselves to Your loving touch. In Jesus' name we pray, Amen.

READ THIS:

"For the Lord seeth not as man seeth; for man looketh on the outward appearance, but the Lord looketh on the heart." 1 Samuel 16:7 (KJV)

DISCUSSION STARTERS:

- Describe an outfit, hairdo, or some area of beauty that makes you feel like things are going to improve or gives you strength to go on.

- When you look into a sister's eyes and see pain, what do you want to do?

- What do you do?

Notes:

_____

_____

_____

_____

_____

_____

_____

_____

_____

_____

_____

_____

_____

_____

_____

_____

_____

_____

_____

_____

_____

_____

_____

_____

_____

_____

_____

_____

_____

_____

_____

_____

Words of Inspiration:

YOU are EVE
awakening the dream
with your glory
especially created to
serve in the image of
excellence
ordained by God to
blow the mind of
a mortal man
WHEN HE FINDS YOU, HE
FINDS HIS:
crowning glory
forgiving heart
soothing comforter
attentive ear
experienced negotiator
broader vision
prayer partner
skilled beautifier
personalized playmate
divine lover
anointed lifesaver
awesome good "thing"

His Good "Thing"

When God makes wives, He doesn't make maids, hags, nags, ball & chain, slaves, old ladies, and let's not even talk about the "B" word. God made us in His image and designed us with a specialty in mind. We are anointed to be the *"ezer kenegdo"* to our mates.

I found out that the Biblical words *"help"* *"meet"* in this scripture means *lifesaver*.[24] God made us to walk alongside and help ward off any attacks that try to come against our mission. God knows what each man needs in order to accomplish the mandate: "Be fruitful and multiply" (Genesis 1:2). Don't think of this just for making babies but think about being fruitful in all other ways, multiplying dreams, ministries, careers, and visions for the family.

Girlfriend Talk

(Gwen) *"My grandmother said that men are like babies. I didn't accept that but I found out how much my husband depends on me for many things. It was an eye opening realization."*

(Renee) *"When I got married, my ideas were nothing like my husband's. As far as I was concerned he was supposed to be my "Prince Charming" and he would understand me and everything I needed. I did everything wrong, girl.*

So I talked to a mother of the church and she gave me the best advice. She said to pray for God to give you wisdom to do what you can do."

* * *

Your perception is different from your husband's. Your emotions are different. Practically everything about you is different and your methods of warfare are different. Come on, you all! We're dangerous if the welfare of our families is threatened.

Walking in your purpose helps your mate develop in the way God has planned for him to develop. God has a purpose for both husband and wife within the marriage that is designed to bless and extend the marriage to a greater level of existence. Walking in purpose gives him the confidence and honor and helps him be himself with you and others. It supports him in his work as he learns how to be the spiritual leader of his home (husbands bring baggage to a marriage too).

Girlfriend Talk

(Barbara) *"I found out that I had to be the administrator and organizer of the family when we were planning our wedding, and it's been that way ever since. I've had to become the CPA, the family banker, Sergeant at Arms and a lot of things. But I don't mind. It's second nature now. I make sure my husband eats properly, takes his medicine on time, and does everything to meet his and the family's needs."*

* * *

God loves both of you and He desires you to be a whole "one." It is in our nature to want to please our mates anyway. So be proud to be somebody's wife. He can't live without you, no matter what he says.

If you are single, know this: You are no less blessed in the eyes of God than a sister who is married. You may be waiting for that day when God will "hook you up" with the man of your dreams. What a privilege you have to get to really know yourself and practice being all that you were designed to be. What a wonderful gift you will be to the man that wins your heart. You have the upper hand girl.

SISTER TIP: Get with some wife friends and bring some hats or make a paper hat for each "hat" you wear. Brag on how well you do things. Single sisters can brag too. You have to wear many hats as well.

Pray Together:

Lord, thank You for the wonderful position we have as women. Whether we're married or not, in Your eyes we're special. Help us to walk into our purposes and our roles prayerfully, lovingly and willingly for Your glory. Show us how not to focus on others failures and faults but on how to be more of what You've made us to be. In Jesus' name we pray, Amen.

READ THIS:

"A virtuous and worthy wife (earnest and strong in character) is a crowning joy to her husband, but she who makes him ashamed is rottenness in his bones."

Proverbs 12:4 (AMPLIFIED BIBLE)

DISCUSSION STARTERS:

- Describe a time when you seriously had second thoughts about being a wife.

- Describe the length of time it took to understand and settle into the position of being a wife.

- How has your description of a wife differed from that of your husband's?

- If you are not married, how are you preparing yourself, (physically; emotionally; and spiritually) for marriage?

Notes:

Words of Inspiration:

A Mothering Wife ...
smothers

A Frustrated Wife ...
complains

A Fearful Wife ...
nags

An Angry Wife ...
argues

A Manipulating Wife ...
cuts off communication

A Depressed Wife ...
gives up

A Praying Wife ...
Believes God

Cause and Effect

For every action there is a source. What is the source of your actions? Are you living in fear, frustration, and anger… or do you believe God's Word for the success of your marriage?

The Bible says that God hears and answers the prayers of His children Psalms 86:7 (my paraphrase.) Over time, we get so comfortable with our spouses that we think we know them inside and out. We know what things they do wrong and what things they do right.

They don't need supernatural intervention, if they would just fix those wrong things, everything would be all right. Right? We reserve prayer for the things for other people and other things.

Girlfriend Talk

(Joy) *"One day, I decided to go back to my hometown to visit my family. This is not something that was planned by my husband. So he said to me, "You don't need to go."*

I said, "Why not?"

My husband said, "Because I am not going." Now the heat is on, and it becomes a submission problem. Me, although not recognizing it has anything to do with submission, I went out of town anyhow.

When I returned from my trip, I got the cold shoulder again, and it was quiet, no communication, except for general comments, and then it falls through the roof. I listened to a lecture and get the Word put on me; that I am not obedient, as the Word of God did say that I am to obey my husband in all things. My thought process at this time is how can you preach the Word to me about obedience, but you are not walking in total obedience yourself, as you are supposed to love me as God loved the church, and loving me right now is not staying angry at me, and giving me the cold shoulder for days, this is not how God does."

* * *

For every action, there is an effect. What are your actions saying? What effects do you see reoccurring in your life? Whatever the situation is, it's not too unyielding for God to turn things around for you. Remember God said He would supply all of our needs. All means ALL. That includes the love we need from our husbands. We simply have to let Him.

Girlfriend Talk

(Joy) *"Through much fasting and praying through the years, and studying the Word of God, (for myself) God has helped me to humble myself and walk in obedience to His will for me to be the help meet He ordained me to be to my husband. I constantly remind myself that I only have to answer to God for the deeds that I have done in my body, how I treat my husband whether I believe he is walking in obedience to God or not."*

* * *

If you are single, pay attention to your reactions now. Find the source and make the necessary adjustments in your decisions. This takes practice.

Use your waiting time to armor up with all the virtue and strength you will undoubtedly need.

> *SISTER TIP: Have a Married Sisters bonfire. Write down all of the expectations that we hold our husbands or others responsible for on a long sheet of paper. Then vow to give these expectations to God in prayer and burn the list.*

Pray Together:

Dear Lord, when it comes to our husbands, we need more faith in your Word. Help us to remember that You are faithful to everyone, including our husbands, and that You do understand our role as wives. Help us to trust You for our marriages and know if we put them in Your hands they will prosper. Alert us through Your Spirit when our reactions show that we're losing our trust. Increase our faith in Your Word. In Jesus' name we pray, Amen.

READ THIS:

"For the weapons of our warfare are not carnal but might through God to the pulling down of strong holds." 2 Corinthians 10:4 (KJV)

DISCUSSION STARTERS:

- What things do you like about your husband?

- What things does your husband do that simply get under your skin?

- What methods have you used to change another person's behavior or actions? Be honest.

- In what ways have you forgiven your husbands for their shortcomings?

Notes:

Words of Inspiration:

Submission
another word for freedom?
you must be joking
hearing it from the pulpit
has an unpleasant sound
like bondage or burden; have enough of
those already
with my hands cracked and peeling from
washing dirty dishes
back straining, neck hurting; cleaning
toilets tired
home from a nine to five, about to take a
nose dive
no
never thought of it as a freedom
but seeing the word like God sees it
makes the picture quite different
"freedom"
to be embraced as a servant of the Lord
to live in fellowship together with God's
Spirit on board
to demonstrate my love for Christ
to enter a gentle spirit; to be a light
to radiate peace and inner stillness
to release stress, live in marital bliss
to accept the Word of God without a fight
as the ultimate authority for my life
not as slave but as a servant
powerful in warfare; praying in fervent
keeping harmony in the home

Submission

I wondered why I almost choked on the word submission every time I heard it. I really didn't want anybody controlling my life especially if that person was unreasonable and inattentive to my needs. The preachers of my day made it quite clear that the concept was spoken by God and was to be obeyed. Still I couldn't wholeheartedly accept it. It seemed unfair and scary. Why did God give women brains if we were not supposed to use them for ourselves? Why does my husband need to lead me? Why doesn't he just lead himself, etc., etc., etc..

Girlfriend Talk

(Renee) *"I thought marriage was a partnership, two people working together as a team. My husband saw wives only as cooks and cleaners. I wasn't a cook, didn't like or want to cook. He wasn't a preacher but he could quote the Bible about submission which made me [seem like] a bad Christian because I didn't do what he wanted me to do. But I knew that I loved God with all of my heart. So most of the time I had hurt feelings."*

* * *

I realized that it wasn't that I'm supposed to submit to a person per se, as much as I am submitting to the Word of God for my life.

God's creation of marriage is a beautiful picture. He wants us to be happy in it. The example before us is Christ and the Church (Eph. 5:22-32). Like Christ, husbands are to love their wives with a sacrificial love. Wives, like the Church, are to submit to/give respect to his direction, his lead and love. (Somebody has to take the lead. A house that is divided will fall.) When this is done like the Word outlines, there is no room for selfishness or self centeredness. Think about your feelings for Christ; how we trust Him for our lives, even when it feels wrong or it's hard to understand. We know that Jesus loves us and we have nothing to fear. We believe that God has our best interest at heart. He will take care of us. So we submit our lives to His direction. God doesn't prohibit us from using our talents, minds and decision-making skills, He provides a better environment for us to use them, (Eph.5:23b).

Ladies, submission is a prerequisite for a great Christian life, married or not. Training our souls to submit to God's leadership is everyone's privilege. It allows the Spirit of God to work on our behalf.

Girlfriend Talk

(Joy) *"I thank God that through His divine intervention, my husband respects my opinion more and is not so headstrong on telling me what I should do or whether I should or should not go anywhere, and does not have the cold-shoulder attitude when we disagree. I have learned to pray and put things in God's hands even before I suggest a trip without him, or any change that could affect our lives. This has made a great difference in my life."*

* * *

Even though your husband may not be perfect like the King of kings look for ways in which he gives his life for you. Working in all kinds of weather to provide for the family and protecting the family even when he may be harmed by doing so, are two examples. I'm sure if you look you'll find more. When we submit, the marriage has a peaceful bliss to it. If you are married to an unsaved husband this may be difficult for both of you to do. It takes the love of Jesus in our hearts to live like the Word instructs. However prayer, respect and counseling will go a long way.

> *SISTER TIP: Have a sister night where you pray for each other's marriages. Chart ways in which your husband sacrifices his life for you and ways that you can show respect and submission to his position as leader accountable to God.*

Pray Together:

Lord, thank You for allowing us to participate in the beautiful creation of marriage. You have provided a vivid portrait of unity between Christ and the Church. Enhance our strength through our femininity, remembering that our submission to your Word makes us powerful warriors in our homes. Renew our desire to walk in fellowship and love together along with you in the Spirit. In Jesus' name we pray, Amen.

READ THIS:

"Finally, be ye all of one mind, having compassion one of another, love as brethren, be pitiful; be courteous: Not rendering evil for evil, or railing fo railing; knowing that ye are thereunto called, that ye should inherit a blessing." 1 Peter 3:8&9 (KJV)

DISCUSSION STARTER

- Describe ways that you exercise submission in your marriage.

- In what ways do you see your husband like the Lord?

- If you are not married, what areas are difficult for you to submit to the Lord?

Notes:

Words of Inspiration:

From tiny explosions to spit fire battles
to feeling like blowing the world apart
things just not working out right
issues mounting up; answers to prayers
riding the local bus

complaint daggers twister speed;
piercing egos of those in its path
from your mouth
fury heating up; steam pushing out
spraying fumes in
quiet storm through the night
while fierce water running down
your cheeks, frustration sets in
anger locked, soul penitentiary

need release, need peace
need a word for the hour

"Be angry and sin not"
the Bible says
no rest in an angry life
calm down; let God work things out

like a lighthouse in a storm
He will light the path
give you direction
and strength for the road
joy comes in the morning
if you let go of the night
passions can bring discord
but God's Word is sharper
than a two edged sword

Fire and Knives

When my husband told me that my angry expressions felt like fire and knives to him, I was shocked and I felt bad. I had no idea it affected him that way because the release felt good to me. I began taking inventory of my reactions. I realized that I don't have the right to throw my frustrations and anger all over him- even though it was he who frustrated me in the first place.

That anger stuff is hard to keep under wraps. It affects your physical, mental, emotional and spiritual being, not to mention your relationships. Every now and then some of it eases out- a fiery look or sharp words. It's lethal.

Girlfriend Talk

(Renee) *"I've always held things in. After my first daughter was born, the doctor told me I shouldn't have any more babies. He said my body couldn't handle more stress, I guess because I wasn't expressing things that bothered me. I think I learned how to hold my anger by watching my grandmother who seemed to be in control of herself all of the time. Unless you knew me, you wouldn't suspect I'm angry. I've learned now to release the stress by communicating quickly. Not looking for the person to change to my wants, I leave that to God. But I get it out of me- in a godly manner."*

* * *

What do you do when there are unresolved issues at hand? Ignoring your feelings doesn't work. Anger and frustration turned inwards becomes depression.

Girlfriend Talk

(Francine) *"I used to 'go off' when I got angry with my husband. But I knew that I couldn't just do that and keep a good testimony as a child of God so I stopped; but I would still be angry inside. I stayed burdened with loads of baggage. I didn't want to minister out of my emotions because I also knew that the anger is what would come out to everyone. It wasn't fair; he made me so angry. He wouldn't do what I wanted him to do. Things were not changing. Finally I got fed up with myself. I found the book, The Power of a Praying Wife, (Stormie Omartin). Her book led me to look to God. When I started trusting God to take care of my concerns, I released everything. Now I feel as light as a butterfly. I still get angry from time to time, that's normal, but now I know where to put it."*

* * *

Most of the time anger hangs around us because we want to solve problems ourselves. We need God to give us a way out- and He does. The Bible says, "Casting all your care upon him; for He careth for you." (1 Peter 5:6-8 KJV). Our trust in God will increase as we give Him our issues to handle. In exchange He'll give us strength to stand as He works on our situations.

Understand that He knows our needs. Taking it to the Lord in prayer doesn't seem like the most effective method of release to the flesh, but when you realize that God has limited himself to work within our prayers, you will see that PRAYER DOES CHANGE THINGS!

Let's take a minute and imagine yourself in the middle of your anger, at the foot of the cross, sitting next to a river of still beautiful water. Calm breezes are gently blowing on your face and Jesus is standing there ready to embrace you with comfort and restoration for your soul. Wouldn't you give your anger to Him? Remember in Psalms 23: 2-3? "He leadeth me by still waters, He restoreth my soul" (KJV). Let God restore your soul over and over through life.

> *SISTER TIP: Find a sister in Christ with whom you can be yourself while you release some of the pressure. Have her pray with you. What are sisters for? Return the favor!*

Pray Together:

Lord, we thank You for knowing how it feels to be angry. Thank You for loving us even when we forget to bring our problems to You for release. Show us how to trust You for our deliverance, even during those hard to trust 'You' times. Remind us to be patient and trust Your Word while we wait for your guidance. In Jesus' name we pray, Amen.

READ THIS:

"For we have not an high priest which cannot be touched with the feeling of our infirmities; but was in all points tempted like as we are, yet without sin. Let us therefore come boldly unto the throne of grace, that we may obtain mercy, and find grace to help in time of need." Hebrews 4:15, 16 (KJV)

DISCUSSION STARTERS:

- Describe a time when your temper made you explode or implode.

- Have you ever carried anger within you for a long time before dealing with it? Why? When and how did you deal with it?

Notes:

Words of Inspiration:

Sometimes we use our mouths
for the wrong reasons
talking out of season
bringing down our soul's displeasin'
even guilty of treason

But if we want a victory sign
our mouths may be the
best weapon at the time
to hinder a spiritual crime

putting satan under our feet
making him flee to safe retreat
canceling his assignment
causing him great discontentment

neutralizing his attacks
making his plans go whack
eradicating the accusations
casting down evil imaginations

empowering us to stand in our liberty
claiming our destiny

So using our mouths for gossip and back
biting is supporting a life that's fallen.
and by the way,
stonewalling' is also missing our mouths'
calling.

Big Beautiful Mouths

If God didn't give women any other gift, he definitely gave us the "gift of gab." We know how to handle our words. We know how to build up and tear down, how to bruise and heal. Our mouths are powerful and they get us in trouble more than anything else does.

James 3:6-8 talks about our tongue being like a fire that's hard to tame. Talking out of turn may not be exclusive to women, but because of our nature, communication plays a great part in relating to each other. The problem is not that we talk, it's how we talk. Nevertheless James 1:19 instructs us to be "swift to hear and slow to speak."

Have you ever said something that you wished you hadn't? Did it seem like it just sort of popped out of you?

Girlfriend Talk

(Barbara) *"I remember when I was eighteen years old, someone had done something that I didn't like. I felt compelled to talk about it to someone else. There I was, reading down this other woman when I noticed that she was in ear shot of everything I was saying. I felt so bad. My grandmother had taught me to let my light shine, and I knew this was not good Christian character. I had to apologize. I decided that I would keep my thoughts to myself until I had prayed about them first."*

(Gwen) "Something like that happened to me too. I was at work and I didn't like the way another teacher treated the children or my friend, her co-teacher. I was telling the cook how I felt and why. Passionately and loudly I talked about this teacher. I was in the middle of my sentence when she walked into the kitchen. I was shocked but I couldn't let the cook suspect that I was really talking behind this teacher's back by cutting off my words, so to cover my embarrassment I had no choice but to address the teacher herself. I was not prepared to confront her, but I played it off. Talking about foot in mouth, I promised myself that I would be more careful about shooting off my mouth."

* * *

The Bible says in Luke 6:45, what's in your heart will come out of your mouth (my paraphrase.) So it's really not a mouth problem. It's a heart problem. If we keep our hearts pure, our mouths will speak words of life and not death. Just think how powerful we'll be against the deception of the devil, armed with truth at the tip of our tongues.

My friend, Francine, says that when she would try to fix things that she had said situations would get all twisted making a bigger mess than before. She finally learned that when people come to her with news, she would simply grab them by the hand and say "let's pray."

Because of its creative ability, the mouth can be both a powerful weapon against the enemy and a source of encouragement to people as well as to ourselves. We are designed to praise God with our mouths. The more we use our mouths for praise, the more our hearts will be filled with good thoughts. It's an everyday thing. Do like our mothers used to tell us, "mind your mouth."

On an opposite note, sometimes our actions speak louder than our words. Ignoring, and willfully not speaking to each other is called stonewalling. Our actions are speaking loudly and clearly what is in our hearts. The best way to mind our mouths is to take our hearts to God for a complete overhaul.

SISTER TIP: Create a "God's Goodness List" and carry it around with you. The next time you or a sister in Christ begins to talk out of control, whip it out and replace the subject with a topic off of the list.

Pray Together:

Lord, thank You for giving us our mouths. What a beautiful and powerful instrument it is. Show us how to speak words of life and not offence. Help us when we get so emotional not to disregard what and how we speak. Direct our words each day. Lord we lift our hearts for you to search them and see if there is any wicked ways there. Give us clean hearts, so that our words will bring glory to Your name. In Jesus' name we pray, Amen.

READ THIS:

"Let no foul or polluting language, no evil word nor unwholesome or worthless talk (ever) come out of your mouth, but only such (speech) as is good and beneficial to the spiritual progress of others as is fitting to the need and the occasion, that it may be a blessing and give grace (God's favor) to those who hear it." Ephesians 4:29 (AMPLFIED BIBLE)

DISCUSSION STARTERS:

- What ways do you manage the words that would come out of your mouth?

- When have you begun to say something and changed it in midstream to something else? Why?

- List ways in which you make your mouth a mouthpiece for God.

Notes:

Words of Inspiration:

Whatever is true
Whatever is worthy of reverence
Whatever is honorable
and seemly
Whatever is lovely
and lovable
Whatever is kind
and winsome
and gracious
if there is any virtue and excellence

if there is
anything worthy of praise
Think on and weigh and take account
of these things

FIX YOUR MINDS ON THEM

* * *

Taken from Philippians 4:8 (AMPLIFIED BIBLE)

This Line of Thought

Women are natural nurturers and many times we think about the needs of our loved ones more than our own. We are aware of almost everything. So we worry; about the house, the husband or our singleness. We worry about our money, the church folks, everything. We tend to dwell on the concerns and issues that we can't do anything about. The Bible says in Proverbs 23:7 that we become what we think (my paraphrase). So if you have worried thoughts, you'll become a worried person. Worriment brings on stress that can lead to physical, emotional, and spiritual problems.

Girlfriend Talk

(Gwen) *"When my eldest son decided he was grown enough to leave home, he found a terrible room in a terrible rooming house close to the college he attended. He and his father wouldn't let me interfere with his male independence, but I was afraid for his safety. To make matters worse, he worked after hours and had to travel in the dark on public transportation.*

Every time I thought about him, my heart would worry, imagining all the things that could happen. When we would see each other, he always had a horror story to tell. He was as happy as a lark. He placed a written statement of faith and safety over his door and decided to trust God for his protection. He didn't worry about anything. I figured he didn't know any better but the truth was that he put his trust in the Word of God on the door. Fortunately he found adequate housing shortly after.

Years later, God showed me a picture of an angel standing on the outside of that door. God had protected him from the start. I had nothing to worry about then, and I know God is still faithful."

* * *

We have the power to change and control what we think about. We can arrest negative thoughts and make them obey the Word of God. Begin by praising God out loud, drown them out with singing. Speak the Word that blows the negative thought right out of your mind. Call a girlfriend and ask them to pray with you. You've got better things to think about.

> *SISTER TIP: Create a "Peace" basket. Put in praise music CDs, soft pillows or stuffed animals, some chocolate candy or hot cocoa (of course) some scripture and anything else that reminds you that God's got it in control. Grab it when needed. Make one for your sister.*

Pray Together:

Lord, thank You for Your goodness and the goodness of others. The unpleasant things in our lives are no match for Your love. Help us to remember and remind each other that our help comes from You. Sometimes our minds race ahead and make us anxious and stressful. We cannot look at the circumstances around us; we have to keep our eyes on You. Lord, You are well able to handle all of our circumstances. Help us to stay focused even when everything in our senses says the opposite. We want to believe Your report about us that we are saved, we are healed and we are whole. In Jesus' name we pray, Amen.

READ THIS:

"Casting down imaginations and every high thing that exalteth itself against the knowledge of God, and bringing into captivity every thought to the obedience of Christ." 2 Corinthians 10:5 (KJV)

DISCUSSION STARTERS:

- Our thoughts determine what we say and how we behave. Describe a time when your negative thinking caused an altercation between you and another person.

- Describe a time when your good thinking brought light to a challenging situation.

Notes:

SOUL CONNECTION

"Each part gets its meaning from the body as a whole, not the other way around. The body we're talking about is Christ's body of chosen people. Each of us finds our meaning and function as a part of His body. But as a chopped-off finger or cut-off toe we wouldn't amount to much, would we?" Romans 12:4-5 Message Bible

This next section explores our connection to the family of God. It is often said; when we draw close to God we automatically draw closer to each other.

Note: This is the largest part of the journey because without our connection to Christ, our journey together is in vain. Open your hearts to the words of inspiration that will come from your travelling buddies. Don't miss any opportunities that God allows to hear His voice.

Words of Inspiration:

When I realize how
magnificent You are
how utterly awesome
how nothing can
 match Your beauty
how few words
spoken from Your mouth
embodies every provision made
before the thoughts of man could
figure it out

my mind explodes within itself
HOLY ART THOU

when I think about how lethal is
Your judgment
how dangerous are Your words
how exclusive are Your thoughts
and the control of Your hand

my being bows down
IN HOLY REVERANCE

when I ponder how:
liberal You are in your giving
brilliant in Your knowledge
majestic in Your being
perfect in Your grace
radiant in Your mercy
original in Your style

grand in Your stand
stately on Your throne

my emotions are captured with the
realization

THAT YOU ARE REALLY GOD

when I consider the
authority of Your name:
Creator; Provider; Victory;
Supplier Covenant;
Healer; Sanctifier;
Righteousness
Peace; Shepherd; Anointing; Lord
I melt in my inadequacy
I CRY HOLY

GOD
how desirable You are
better than gold
sweeter than honey

YEAH!
and the honeycomb

Praise

We serve an awesome God who wants to connect with us on a personal level. His names alone indicate that He is everything to us. He can be as big as we need Him to be and little enough to fit in to those tiny issues in our lives. He fills every area.

Girlfriend Talk

(Gwen) *"Back when Heather and I were only sisters in church together, in the ladies' room, she accidentally smashed her little daughter's fingers in the bathroom door. And as most mothers would, she quickly and passionately began to soothe them. I was intrigued when she broke into a prayer for her daughter's fingers. The prayer was a surprise to me. After all it wasn't a bad smash just a quick slight one, not big enough to get the almighty God involved, right? She was unaware that I was watching, but I never forgot it! Now that we're girlfriends and spend a lot more quality time together, I've had plenty opportunities to watch her include God in almost every insignificant area of her life. From losing weight to finding a good bra, no area seemed to be excluded. I didn't have that. Even though I loved God with all of my heart, I'd always reserved the little concerns for myself to handle. As we talked about this, she reminded me about the scripture in Luke 12:7. God is so in touch with us that he has numbered the hairs on our heads."*

* * *

You can't get more insignificant than that! On one hand, I knew God knows everything about us; after all, He is God. But to understand that He wants to be involved with every part our lives, even our hair, makes it an awesome love story. Who even cares about the number of the hairs on our heads anyway? God does.

Remember who loves you. Think about Him all day long. Watch Him work in your life – making ways where there is no way. Magnify Him at every turn. All through the day, think of His goodness. Thinking about God keeps us in peace and reminds us that we can do all things through him. Be intimate with Him all day long and watch the difference.

> *SISTER TIP: What are girlfriends for? We make a difference in each other's lives like Heather made in my life. So share your God experiences with one of your girlfriends. If you don't have a girlfriend yet, find a sister in Christ and share with her.*

Pray Together:

Lord, we are humbled in your presence. Saying "Thank You" cannot adequately express our praise to You. But we keep trying because You are marvelous in our eyes. Words alone fail us. So we lift our gifts, our talents our lives to You to do with us what you will. You're so wonderful that even though we're giving gifts to You we're blessed by the giving. Thank You for loving us so much. Lead us, guide us and show us Your heart. We want you to be front and center in our lives. All our praise and glory goes to You. In Jesus' name we pray, Amen

READ THIS:

"Yours, O Lord, is the greatness and the power and the glory and the victory and the majesty, for all that is in the heaven and the earth is Yours;

Yours is the kingdom, O Lord, and Yours it to be exalted as Head over all."
I Chronicles 29:11(NKJV)

DISCUSSION STARTERS:

- In what areas of your life do you unintentionally exclude God? How about intentionally?

- Describe an incident in your life in which you didn't fully see God's hand, His direction or His will.

Notes:

Words of Inspiration:

When I'm with the Saints
our arms raised in jubilation
voices tied in harmony
feet hot in the shout
minds on one accord
hearts brimming with joy
ears anticipating God's directions
Eyes seeing the answers to prayers
Souls filled with adoration
Faces covered in contentment
Hope strengthened
Faith activated
Discouragement turned to confidence
Understanding made clear
Loneliness replaced with fulfillment
Fears taken over by the peace of God
Sadness changed to rejoicing
Tiredness to celebration
and burdens lifted
When I'm with the Saints,
IT'S BETTER THAN:
Eating popcorn at the movies
Watching football on T.V.
Playing a game of checkers
Taking an easy day
Washing the car... Petting
animals at the zoo
Hosting a barbecue
Hanging out with friends staying at home
Cleaning the house or riding on a roller coaster.
When I'm with the Saints.

When I'm with the Saints

The anointing of the Lord rests heavily on the atmosphere when saints come together in one place with time devoted specifically to praising and hearing from God. This is different from when the Lord speaks to you on a personal level. How would you feel if a group of people laid aside everything they were doing to come together and hear what you had to say? Wouldn't you want to prepare something special for them?

The blessings from God are priceless and irreplaceable. Satan tries to keep us alone so he can have our minds all to himself. Sometimes the last thing you want to do at the end of a hard day is go to church and smile with more people. But out of sheer obedience or guilt, you drag yourself there. To your surprise, you leave feeling refreshed, encouraged and glad you went.

Girlfriend Talk

(Candace) *"When my mother asked me to attend a women's Bible study, I talked myself into it by saying, I should go because I need more people in my life. Now I'm glad because it helped me to grow and see more of who I am. I feel comfortable talking to other ladies now. I actually feel safe and enhanced in my relationship with God. I was not comfortable with sharing, just relating to people at all. I'm not really an open person. Life would have been lonely and everything would feel like it was my fault. Now I look forward to going, laughing, sharing, and praying. I try not to miss a class."*

(Renee) "I remember I had the flu and I felt so bad, I didn't want to go to church. I went anyway, but I didn't want anybody to say anything to me. I just wanted to be alone. At the end of service, a woman who was a new member and whose son had a disability, handed me a Christmas card. She said she didn't have money to buy a gift, but she wanted me to know that she thanks God every day for bringing me into her life. She said that my ministry had changed her life. I thought, even though I wasn't well, this was worth the trip."

* * *

Now, I know you can get the Word of God preached to you by listening online and watching television, but what about the fellowship? Coming together gives us a chance to walk out the principles of loving each other. It is difficult or nearly impossible to love people like Christ instructs us to, without spending time together. When brothers and sisters grow up together in the same house, there is a bonding that happens that connects them in deep ways. The Lord instructs us to encourage each other, forgive, forbear, and to be patient with each other. The "what's in it for me" principle does not exist in God's model of love. Even when everybody doesn't demonstrate the best example of Christian living, it gives us practice in loving the unlovely and provides a reason for intercessory prayer on that person's behalf.

Going to church is like filling up at a gas station. Getting together with people who love God refreshes you and gives strength to praise your way out of adversities. I can encourage your heart in your weak area and you can do the same for me. When I see others connecting to the glory of God, it makes me want to get in the praise too. Do you have anything to offer a sister? You never know what a blessing your presence may be to someone else.

Worldly fun is no substitute for the glory of God. Peace, joy and love cannot be purchased! The Bible tells us that one can chase a thousand, and two can put ten thousand to flight (Deuteronomy 32:30). I like to think of that scripture in terms of chasing demons and depressing spirits. No wonder the enemy doesn't want us to get together.

SISTER TIP: Listen to your sister, DON'T MISS CHURCH! Call as many sisters as you can when you miss them attending church service.

Pray Together:

Lord, You said in Your Word where two or three are gathered together in Your name, You are there. Thank You for brothers and sisters, who love us, support us, hold us up in prayer and encourage us. Thank You for the opportunity to be known and to know others. Binding up fear and embracing patience with each other, help us to reach out in loving connections. Thank You for a family of saints. In Jesus' name we pray, Amen.

READ THIS:

"Not forsaking or neglecting to assemble together (as believers) as is the habit of some people but admonishing (warning, urging and encouraging) one another and all the more faithfully as you see the day approaching." Hebrews 10:2 (AMPLIFIED BIBLE)

DISCUSSION STARTERS:

- Describe what started your habit of attending church services.

- Other than illness or transportation related reasons, what are some of the reasons you might have skipped attending some church services?

- Describe a time when you unexpectedly received a blessing from a sister or brother when you attended a church service.

- Describe friendships that developed for you as a result of your connections at church.

Notes:

Words of Inspiration:

Tornadoes twirling
about my feet
bells ringing in my ears
Spirit surrounding me
uncontrollable joy
whistling on air
above the shadows

to honor Him.. leaping
King of kings
Lord of lords

to praise His holy name
for victory over the enemy
for His exclusive pleasure

to honor him.. shouting
Glorious Father
Prince of Peace

I lay down my inhibitions
and offer up my comfort in
TOTAL PRAISE

Dance

There are moments in our lives when you have to dance; a simple cheer just won't do. The same applies to praising God. There's a praise that connects your soul to the glory of God that is so powerful it makes you want to dance in order to express it. At home, I'd cut a step in praise at the spin of a CD, but don't ask me to do it at church. I was too self-conscious of what others would think.

Girlfriend Talk

(Gwen) *"During one such praise-fest at home, the Lord impressed me to release my praise dance the next time I praised Him in church, telling me that dancing for God was the most complete physical form of praise. It involves your whole body. I thought, 'Interesting.' I wasn't prepared for the next thing He said, 'Do you love me enough to humiliate yourself for my sake?' After I repented for putting my self-pride above my love for Him, I promised that I would dance for Him in the public eye. I can't say that the experience didn't feel funny but so what? When I think of how Jesus made Himself a public spectacle on Calvary for my sake, it makes me wanna dance! I've been dancing for Him ever since."*

* * *

For some of us moving our bodies could be an act of faith; especially if we have long past the running and jumping for fun stage. I believe the physical act of praise commands the flesh to subject itself to God.

Sometimes you have to dance in faith for deliverance. Dancing in joy for the answer to your prayer before the answer comes is a strong testimony of faith to God. Today, why don't you praise God in "the dance." You don't have to be in church. Wherever you are, cut a step. I like to dance around the coffee table at home. Go ahead, you'll feel the release. Wouldn't it be nice to have a dancing partner? Party hearty!

> *SISTER TIP: Choose a partner and have a victory dancing session. Take turns dancing for each other's blessings past, present and future.*

Pray Together:

Lord, thank You for the privilege of dancing before You. Praise You for the awesome ability to move our hands, our feet, our heads and our bodies as a whole in selfless praise. Not just the physical act of dance but for our spirit that dances before You at any time even in restful times. Help us to always offer holy heartfelt dance in total praise to You; especially during those times when we don't feel like it. That's when it's a sacrifice of praise. Help us not to be more conscience of others than we are of You. Lord, You've done so much for us. We could never praise You too much. In Jesus' name we pray, Amen.

READ THIS:

"Let them praise His name in chorus and choir and with the (single or group) dance." Psalms 149:3 (AMPLIFIED BIBLE)

DISCUSSION STARTERS:

- David danced his clothes off for God. How comfortable are you dancing before the Lord?

- Before Christ, were you a closet dancer or a public dancer?

- Before Christ, what was your favorite dance? Why?

- How has it changed after you've given your life to God.

Notes:

Words of Inspiration:

The world seems full of inspirational gurus
today
who write, speak and tell you what to say
syllables and sounds that play
on your emotions

some thoughts lead you down a path
disappointing at the end
talk show hosts make the most
out of cheers and applause, a deceptive
blend

masquerading a false hope
demonic midwives aborting the truth
so real in its counterfeit
drawing souls in its kaleidoscope

but thank God for Jesus
who died to give me diamonds of life
who died to keep me from living in strife

who died to offer me vitality
my longevity, more abundantly
through Him I live, breathe and have my
being

He is genuine, He is authentic
there is no other like Him
JESUS IS REAL

Keeping It Real

Turn the television on at almost any time, and you're apt to see advice givers. Each one has a different price, a different motive, a different slant and a different reason for their chosen profession. Which one would you choose for help? I don't know about you, but when I'm hurting, confused and need instruction, I want to talk to somebody who loves me, who wants the best for me and who knows me.

Jesus is that somebody. He knows our destinies; He knows what's within us. Not only does He know how many times we make the same mistakes over and over, but also He knows why and what is needed to stop the process.

Girlfriend Talk

(Kim) *"I had issues with purity. I couldn't do it. I was a member in good standing at my church, but when it came down to it, I was also a whore. I wasn't the only one. My friends were dealing with the same issue.*

The subject wasn't addressed at church even though they all knew that sex outside of marriage was against the Ten Commandments. It was as if it was ignored or something. I didn't think living pure could be done. But something inside me kept searching for the real answer. I struggled inside wanting to do what was right. My battle got worse the more I tried to live right. I didn't want to be like everybody else. I didn't want to go to hell because of anything, but especially not because of sex.

I was excited when the announcement went out that a visiting speaker was coming to speak about purity. Her testimony was awesome. You name it, and she had done it. She wasn't shy or safe about it; she told it like it was. She aggressively brought the delivering message of Jesus Christ right to me it seemed. Yes! You Can Live Pure Before Marriage! Jesus knew my heart and what I needed. He came to my rescue bringing the real truth. I made a decision that night. I was going to do whatever it took to live pure before God. As I changed my life patterns and put Him first by reading His Word and spending time with Him in prayer, my life choices changed. Now I can say I am victorious in this battle. AMEN!

* * *

Jesus is real. He won't take advantage of us or lead us down a wrong path. He brings truth to every subject and every concern. John 8:32 says, "Ye shall know the truth and the truth shall make you free." Meditate on God's Word for your concerns. Get the right answer! Allow Jesus to speak His Word into your heart. Purchase one of those little books that have scriptures listed for every situation. Spend some time with the answers. Get it out of your mind and make it audible in words. Speak the Word out loud so you can hear it coming from you.

> SISTER TIP: Discuss the popular talk shows on air these days. Get together and pray for the participants that have been on the shows with serious relational and family problems.

Pray Together:

Dear Lord, in this world that is full of trickery and deception, thank You for being the true and living God. Help us not to get sidetracked by false advisors or even to trust our own reasoning. Just as You are truthful with us help us to be honest with ourselves and

then with You. Speak to us as we come to You for daily help. You promised that if we seek You, we'll find that You are ready to help us. In Jesus' name we pray, Amen.

READ THIS:

"Blessed (happy, fortunate, prosperous, and enviable) is the man who walks and lives not in the counsel of the ungodly (following their advice, their plans and purposes), nor stands (submissive and inactive) in the path where sinners walk, nor sits down (to relax and rest) where the scornful (and mockers) gather." Psalms 1:1 (AMPLIFIED BIBLE)

DISCUSSION STARTERS:

- Why do you think people do not go to the church for advice as much as they may go elsewhere?

- In your opinion, how real is a psychic?

- What's the difference between being "churchy" and "real"?

Notes:

Words of Inspiration:

Blessings are like supernatural bubbles
purposely floating around, lighting on our
heads at the command of the Almighty;
Him knowing our intentions before they are
conceived,
thinking the best for us.
He dispatches them at will

Some we get to keep us going like a flu
shot in the winter.
Some like presents in a surprise birthday
party with balloons, wonderful and unexpected.
Some are like family reunions reminding us
of who we are.
Some feel good like watching a dancer's
twirl, filling our hearts with awe.
Some bring laughter to your belly,
satisfying like a peanut butter and jelly.
Blessings are nice
like apple pie a la mode, meeting and
mixing with filling most scrumptious.
Blessings are aggressive,
chasing behind you; running you down;
getting in front of you and waiting 'till you
catch up,
Only to Chase You Down Again
A Blessing is knowing my unworthiness
and seeing God's love for me
Blessings from prayers uttered during
tearful moments, long ago forgotten; then
answered.

THAT'S A BLESSING!

Blessings

Do you want to put a damper on feeling bad? Start counting your blessings. It's a full-time pleasure. How wonderful it is to know you're blessed of God.

It's easy to forget what God has done for us when things are looking down. The emotions have a lot to do with that. Feelings have a way of interfering with the thoughts and swaying them in their direction. But when we pay attention to our blessings, it's an eye opener and a mind blower. Our emotions don't have a chance against the good things of God in our lives. Dwell on them.

Girlfriend Talk

(Gwen) *"The other day, I confess, I looked back at my life and started counting the wrong things; all the struggles, the hurt feelings, the crazy situations, the stuff I messed up, the things and people I failed, the projects I dropped. It was enough to dip into a great depression. But to my surprise, I discovered God's incredible grace. That in spite of all I've been through, God has blessed me better than I could have done even without the problems. Looking back, I saw where I should have failed in every way, but God kept me. What a surprise!"*

(Renee) *"I was puzzled because I wondered why my son was having so much trouble graduating from high school. It bothered me, being a teacher and all.. But somehow God opened my eyes and showed me the big picture. Some children just have a harder time at doing some things than others. This was hard for him but in some other things he would do great. That little thought made me relax about him graduating and he did. That's a blessing."*

* * *

It surprises us to see how much God has done for us, big and little. You like surprises don't you? Connect with God in gratitude for all He's done in your life. Tell somebody else. Count them up! You go girl!

> SISTER TIP: *Have a night when you and your sister company count your blessings using jelly beans. Every sister gets a bunch and has to talk about God's blessings while disposing of the jelly beans until all are gone. (You don't have to eat them. You can find another way to get rid of them).*

Pray Together:

Lord, when we think of Your goodness, we can't begin to thank You enough. Thank You, Thank You, and Thank You. Even when we haven't a clue, You are still blessing us. We realize that we haven't earned them or deserved them. Knowing that Your favor is not given as payment for good deeds or good behavior but just because You love us. That makes us more grateful for Your wonderful love. In Jesus' name we pray, Amen.

READ THIS:

"The blessing of the Lord, it maketh rich and he addeth no sorrow with it." Proverbs 10:22 (KJV)

DISCUSSION STARTERS:

Make a list of God's Regular and/or Special blessings.

- Make a list of blessings that were surprises.

- Encouraging blessings

- Validating blessings

- Mind blowing blessings

- Answered prayers

Notes:

Words of Inspiration:

To
Breathe
Breath
from
God
each
one
Authored
and
Ordained
Intentionally
Personalized!

Privileged

When someone is called "privileged," we assume that they are afforded certain opportunities in life that the average person cannot have. What category do you fit in? Think about this morning. How did you feel when you took a deep breath, that first full yawn and stretch? Did you know that you filled your lungs with fresh, unused air and detoxified your body from last night's stale air? By the time the oxygen passes through the veins and fibers of your body, a magnificent job was already done. God knows how many breaths you will take to live out your life, and He authors and protects each one. It's the serving and knowing a God so awesome, yet so personal that is the privilege. We don't even notice we're breathing most of the time. Yet not one breath goes unnoticed by God. We haven't done anything to earn this privilege, truth be told we've done many things that should disqualify us from receiving such love.

Girlfriend Talk

(Gwen) *"After Sunday evening services, I suddenly realized that I struggled for each breath. The deeper I tried to inhale, the less air would come. Of course I knew what to do. I called my praying sisters present at the church. They prayed right then without stopping until suddenly, after about twenty or thirty minutes I began to successfully take a deep breath. Do I have to tell you how grateful I was to breathe? Approximately less than a year later, according to my doctor, an EKG uncovered that I had suffered a minor heart attack! I had not even realized it but nothing takes God by surprise. He had already provided the answer for my healing and deliverance!"*

* * *

If God takes that much care in orchestrating each breath, think about everything else in *our* bodies- our lives. Just think about that!

> *SISTER TIP: Get together and do some deep breathing exercises after a hard, long day at work or with the children or whatever may stress you. It relaxes your body and your mind. Praise God for every exhalation.*

Pray Together:

Lord, You are magnificent! When we take the time and think about how good You are to us, we will agree wholeheartedly that we are privileged women. We are so honored to be Your children. We see and feel Your complete love for us and for that we say thank You for thinking about us and loving us on every level. Help us not to take Your grace and mercy for granted. But remind us to accept and honor Your presence in each area of our lives. In Jesus' name we pray, Amen.

READ THIS:

"For in Him we live and move and have our being; as even some of your (own) poets have said. For we are also His offspring." Acts 17:28 (AMPLIFIED BIBLE)

DISCUSSION STARTERS:

- List the number of things you sometimes take for granted in the course of a day.

- When thinking about all the areas that we manage in our lives, which area seems the most insignificant to you?

Notes:

Words of Inspiration:

With the help of a song
I begin my journey to the answers of the
day
the directions to my life
the affirmations of my soul
the peace of my mind
the joy of my season
the quiet in my spirit
the pathway to my destiny
the roads of my ministry
the sense in my world
the guide to my prosperity
the oil for my healing
the keys to my future

on bended knees
the throne doors fly open to me
the King of Kings and Lord of Lords
the Omniscience of the universe with his
Omnipotent voice
that can smash mountains, incite tidal
waves
and swallow up the earth whole
whispers to me

"let's talk"

Prayer Closet

A prayer closet is a designated place that you've decided to meet God. It feels like it shuts the rest of the world out. Mine used to be in the bathroom when the children were young. Now it's in the living room early in the morning or late at night. This place is not for the casual greeting time of morning or evening prayers, it's for quality time set aside to express your love for God and His to you. It's the time when you really want to hear His voice, when you want to "hang out" with God.

Don't substitute prayer time alone with God for other kinds of prayer time with others or in church. You need your own personalized time with God. He will tell you things that are only for you to hear at that time. Don't miss out on that.

Girlfriend Talk

(Aisa) *"It's the place I feel the most safe, comfortable and confident."*

(Kim) *"I didn't have a prayer life before I started putting the Word of God in me. It built up over a period of time. My life is getting stronger and I learn something different every day. I talk to God like I talk to anybody. I'm just myself."*

* * *

David says in Psalms 27: 11, "… lead me in a plain path…." God has all the right answers and He has no problem leading you to them. God will even set up circumstances to spend time with us. He loves our company.

Girlfriend Talk

(Gwen) *"I used to think that the directions that God gave me during these special times were suggestions. But then I found out the things He was telling me were His wisdom. He was saving me time and energy as I went about my life's dealings."*

(Kim) *"I found out it's more about relationship. I act like I'm in love or something. I stay longer than I planned."*

(Joann) *"One time, a family member, gave me the opportunity to use his timeshare property for a weekend at no cost. I didn't want to go alone, so I asked several of my friends and other family members to go with me. Most couldn't go and the ones that said they would didn't for one reason or another. I thought; who would pass up a free trip in the mountains? I ended up going alone anyway. By the second day, I realized that God wanted me there alone so He could talk to me and bless me without any interruptions. The things He showed me, even nature were a testimony of His splendor to me. I came back refreshed, strengthened, rested and encouraged to fully live my life."*

* * *

It's awesome that God Almighty would even want to talk with us. But Psalms 139:17 says that His thoughts about us are precious and more than sand, (my paraphrase).

If you haven't gotten a prayer closet yet, establish a time and a place for the two of you to meet regularly. I guarantee that God will meet you there every time.

SISTER TIP: Do you need to work on this? Get a couple of prayer partners to team up with you at a designated time. Make yourself accountable to them.

Pray Together:

Lord, thank You for being our compass through life. Nobody can direct us, know us better than we know ourselves and love us like You can. Even when we are not consistent in meeting You each day You're always in place waiting for us. Lord, remind us never to give up our time together. Help us remember that You love us and want to spend time with us, waiting patiently for us, even while we're sleeping. Thank You for Your grace and mercy. In Jesus' name we pray, Amen.

READ THIS:

"Let us then fearlessly and confidently and boldly draw near to the throne of grace (the throne of God's unmerited favor to us sinners, that we may receive mercy(for our failures) and find grace to help in good time for every need (appropriate help and well timed help, coming just when we need it)." Hebrews 4:16 (AMPLIFIED BIBLE)

DISCUSSION STARTERS:

- What aspect of prayer do you most enjoy? Why?

- Give an example of a time when you sensed God talking to you during prayer. How did it bless you, or protect you Tell about the time God has awakened you for prayer.

- Describe a time when you might have felt silly praying about something. Why?

Notes:

Words of Inspiration:

Spiritual Consciousness
brand new existence
survival adamant
hunger instinctive,
I'm developing a mind to go on
"Like baby: "I cry for food"

Thriving
nurtured endurance
developing a fortified testimony
hunger necessary
I just want to make it in
Like child: "bread of heaven feed me 'till I
want no more"

Striving
for lasting joy
for perfect peace...
for witnessing power
for standing ability
hunger preferred,
I'm determined to go all the way
Survival is still adamant
Like grown up: "I esteem His words
higher than my necessary food"

Basic Like Food

When it comes to survival, food and water are as basic as it comes. Everybody knows that you have to eat to live. But when it comes to our spiritual side, we sometimes think survival is more complicated.

Girlfriend Talk

(Kim) *"When my mother was diagnosed with Diabetes, I realized I was tricking myself when it came to my diet. I thought I was healthy because I was a vegetarian. But who ever heard of a fat vegetarian? It's like an oxymoron. I'd load up on foods that in excess would bring me where my mother was. I had to pay attention to what I was eating if I expected to be healthy. It's as simple as that! My mom started to change her diet and started exercising. Now the doctors have taken her off of medication and she acts like she is younger than me."*

* * *

Kim taught me that our bodies crave for real food. When we give our bodies real food, instead of processed or junk food, we feel a lasting satisfied feeling.

Claude Fischler, sociologist with the French National Center for Scientific Research asks, "If you are what you eat, and you don't know what you're eating, do you know what you are?"[1] Physically for years I've been anemic and my diet supported it. I would walk into a coffee shop and become engulfed with aromas of fresh brewed hot coffee and sweet donuts. It felt like I just couldn't help indulging.

So it is with our spiritual lives when our spiritual diet consists mostly of the "trash" from the world, we become weak and in danger of falling from grace, anemic. The trash from this world cannot satisfy our spirits. We love God but often we find ourselves losing when we're in a spiritual battle. Have you ever wondered why you may go through so many bouts of depression or sadness or anger? Could it be that your spirit is weak and hungry for spiritual food?

Girlfriend Talk

(Gwen) *"My mind goes in overdrive when I miss praying and reading the Bible. I have so much I want to do in the course of a day and I get frustrated when things do not fall in place the way I want them to. So I begin reasoning heavily, trying to figure out the proper course of action instead of allowing God to lead me and direct my actions. I usually become tired and ultimately depressed especially when my new plans fail- just where Satan wants me to be. I find it easier to remember when I make it a routine like eating a natural meal."*

* * *

"God wants His Word to become the essence of your everyday life."[1] The Bible calls the Word of God bread. Our spirit needs to connect with God at least once on a daily basis. It's as simple as that. Not only will you enjoy it; after a while you'll crave it. Talking to God and reading the Word of God is food for the soul. Are you hungry?

SISTER TIP: *Compare study notes with a sister in Christ. Have you found a scripture or received a clearer illumination from the Word today? Share it!*

Pray Together:

Lord, when we get so bogged down with our lives, we may not feed our spirit like we ought to. Because of that poor nutrition, we suffer bouts of frustration, depression and many other side effects. But we thank You for always reminding us to eat and drink from Your life-giving fountain. Lord we know there is no shortage; we can freely receive from You. Lord we want to always experience hunger and thirst for You. You said that we would be filled. Filled us with Your Word, Your love, Your joy, Your peace. In Jesus' name we pray, Amen.

READ THIS:

"Blessed and fortunate and happy and spiritually prosperous (in that state in which the born-again child of God enjoys His favor and Salvation) are those who hunger and thirst for righteousness (uprightness and right standing with God), for they shall be completely satisfied." Matthew 5:6 (AMPLIFIED BIBLE)

DISCUSSION STARTERS:

- Describe a time when you've noticed feelings or thoughts returning that you had believed you'd conquered.

- Describe a time or times when God enlightened you on a matter during your quiet time of meditation.

- Describe a time when you sensed that your spirit was hungry for the Word or for spending time with God.

Notes:

Words of Inspiration:

Song of Solomon,
Take me away on the breath of His melody
to inhale His fragrance
away from drama too heavy for me to lift
above life's mineshafts hidden from plain
sight
vacationing in His voice. Soothing

Song of Solomon,
Take me away where Jesus is my lover
wrapped in His anointing fire
fulfilling me with His desire
completing me with His rest.
Ahhh...

Rest

Still waking up tired after a long night's rest? Is it because your mind is full of unresolved issues? Or is your soul tired from dealing with life? Are you waking up prematurely through the night? Or are you unable to sleep at all? Are you always hungry? Or is your appetite all but gone? Are you easily aggravated? Or are you almost void of feeling? All of these conditions can be signs of a restless mind. Jesus died to give us rest.

Most of the time, we're overwhelmed and tired because we try to handle things on our own. Some circumstances we've brought on ourselves, others we've inherited. God never meant for us to handle them alone. God provided a package deal that covers us completely against anything that can be a detriment to us. Even when we are guilty of messing things up, there is grace of mercy available for us. All we have to do is ask. When Jesus died on the cross, He became our perfect sacrifice against sin, shame and guilt. Isaiah 53:5 tells us that He was wounded for the sins we would commit. And, He was bruised for the sins of our fathers that would attach themselves to us, and then everything that would chase away our peace, He literally took on Himself and for sickness whether stress related or not the stripes on His back contains our healing, (my paraphrase).

Regardless of the state of your affairs, knowing and trusting that God has already given you the victory, given rest. So let go of your control, God's got it under His control.

Girlfriend Talk

(Renee) *"I was worried because I believed I brought a bad marriage on myself. Living in a bad marriage is like living in hell on earth. My biological clock was ticking, so finding a husband was on the top of my list. When I met my husband, he reminded me of my grandfather, strong, decisive and a regular churchgoer. But afterwards in the marriage, I found out he was much different and I started considering a way out. First, I repented for not listening for God's directions. Back and forth I prayed about whether or not I should stay married. Finally God told me to make a decision in my heart. Was I going to stay or leave? I decided to stay. I knew that God was faithful in answering my prayers for a good marriage. The way I rested was, while I put my faith to work, I prayed over everything. I had specific days to fast for my household and I anointed my husband while he was asleep, his shoes, his clothes, even my own body. I asked God to bring good influences around him in friendship. I put it all in the hands of God and didn't worry. It didn't take two days but I was determined to wait on God. Now my husband is my pastor and God is blessing both of our ministries."*

* * *

It's amazing how God will give us the strength to be at peace even when things have not yet worked out. Hebrews 4:5 says that we have a high priest that knows our infirmities, (my paraphrase). Yes, Jesus understands the hurt, the confusion, the sadness, the pain.

In the middle of the storm God can and will give you rest. David says in Psalms 23:4, "He prepares a table before me in the presence of my enemies." That's just awesome! So why not release yourself to God's complete rest. He will give you directions on how to handle your circumstances. He'll give you a "second wind." You probably need one right about now. Relax your shoulders, loosen your jaws, take a deep breath and think about God who has your best interest in His heart. Think about His power and His ability to make things right. Trust Him. The rest comes in the trusting. No better rest.

SISTER TIP: Do you know a sister that has been worrying about things lately? Or maybe she has had a rough week due to circumstances beyond her control? Put a care basket together for her that includes a soothing Christian CD, some scented flowers, a soft teddy, some resting scriptures and some comfort food. Surprise her with a hug and a prayer as you hand her the basket.

Pray Together:

Lord, thank You for complete rest in Your Word and through Your Spirit. Remind us of times past when we experienced Your deliverance; that You care for us like a father watches his children; that nothing happens without Your knowing eyes. If You did it before You can do it again. Show us whether our unrest is a call to strengthen our faith so that we will remain in Your rest. We open our hearts to You in trust. We let it all go. In Jesus' name we pray, Amen.

READ THIS:

Casting all your cares upon him: for He careth for you. 1 Peter 5:7 (KVJ)

DISCUSSION STARTERS:

- How difficult is it to totally give to God your issues concerning other people's actions?

- Describe a time when you've separated working for God from working for the church or church people.

- Once you've given your problems to God, how difficult is it to leave them there, even when things seem worst?

Notes:

Words of Inspiration:

SUBDUED
by the gravity of a million destinies
POWERED OVER
by the sound of a billion voices
INFERIOR
under the weight of a trillion concerns
SPARKLED OUT
by the fire of a zillion passions
OVER SHADOWED
by the importance of a katrillion lives
Undetected, Unnoticed, Unobserved
a cry as faint as leaves blowing away
OVERFLOWS the heart of God
a problem as easy as daydreams
EXPANDS in the vision of God
a prayer as quiet as falling snow
RESOUNDS in the ear of God
a being as small as a sparrow—me
PRIORITY in the mind of God

Watching

When I think of all the people in the world, I'm astounded by the fact that God even knows that I exist. One day, I was sitting in my car waiting for someone when a little bird pecked around under some bushes close by. I didn't see any other birds around. It was as if it had wandered off from the flock and had gotten lost. To me the bird seemed so small compared to the rest of the world (cars and trucks speeding by and people's conversations as they walked along the way.) I thought, *no one has noticed that the bird was left alone to fend for itself. Who would hear its little chirps? If it gets in trouble who would help?*

I imagined that we are, to a large extent, like that bird. So much of life just speeds by. There are periods that we feel left out, left behind and insignificant.

But regardless of our feelings at any given time we can be confident that God knows us. He knows our whereabouts, and our circumstances. He loves us and hears us when we cry to Him. He never ignores us, ever. He's always with us, even when we find ourselves in compromising situations.

Girlfriend Talk

(Gwen) *"During a particularly difficult financial time in my life, I made a bad decision. I wrote a check hoping I would make a deposit in time to catch* *it before it was returned. The check was for a small grocery bill about $30.00. Unfortunately with so much going on in my life at the time, I forgot I had written it and the market decided to prosecute. We had recently moved and I didn't receive the notices that would have reminded me to pay the check. So over the course of time I received a phone call from the police department telling me to turn myself in for arrest.*

It was an interesting experience I never want to experience again! But the hand of my "Big Daddy" God was visible during the whole ordeal. He moved on the officer's heart when they took me to be fingerprinted. Looking at me he could tell I was inexperienced. So he kept me close to him away from being sent back to the holding cell. Then he asked an attendant for my file which was on the bottom of a very large stack of files, and placed it on the top. Later I found out that the stack was the cases that would be heard that day until 4:00 pm. The rest would have to wait until the next day to be heard. My case wouldn't have been heard until the next day. I would have had to spend the night in jail! Thanks to God I was out of there in about two hours."

Technically, I should have trusted in God for my finances instead of writing a bad check. But fear had led me to do what I believed I had to do at the time. Wrong! God promises to take care of us in every way. We have to trust His care. Sometimes, we learn through our negative experiences. Even though I went through that ordeal, because of His love I learned that He is faithful to His promises. We're never alone.

Think about it as you go about your daily work. Think about how God is looking out for you. In His Word He tells that He crowns us with loving kindness and tender mercies, (Psalms 103:4).

> *SISTER TIP: God really loves you. You must be something special, girl! Be proud to know Jesus. Get together and go to the Christian book store and purchase some tee shirts or sweat shirts that have slogans printed on them about loving the Lord. Wear the message, live the message, share it.*

Pray Together:

Lord God we thank you for your promise never to leave us alone, to be with us at every turn. Lord, there are days when we feel like no one knows our names. We feel all alone and insignificant. But just like the sparrow, You are looking out for us. Lord, when our world seems to be turned sideways, remind us that we can walk with confidence because You love us. We can look up, look around us, look ahead of us and there You are. Thank You for the realization that we belong to You. In Jesus' name we pray, Amen.

READ THIS:

The Lord is my Light and my salvation- whom shall I fear or dread? The Lord is the Refuge and Stronghold of my life- of whom shall I be afraid. Psalms 27:1 (AMPLIFIED BIBLE)

DISCUSSION STARTERS:

- Describe a time when you didn't realized that God was watching and working within your actions or circumstances.

- Describe a time when even though you knew God was with you, it didn't feel like it.

Notes:

Words of Inspiration:

Stripes sliced his back
Thorns punctured his head
Hair yanked out of his face
Pain etched on his brow
Beaten unrecognizable
Battered, banged about, brutalized
blood mixed in every cry
nailed,
hammered
and died for you and me
RISEN IN TOTAL VICTORY!

With Me in Mind

When Asia was battling cancer, to keep from becoming dependent on pain medication, she opted to deal with the pain. That created another problem. Her body was so traumatized by the level of the pain that she also suffered a stroke. Thank God, He miraculously healed her from the stroke and today she is cancer free! Sickness is stressful, not only on your body but on your mind. When you're sick beyond the customary cold or sinus trouble etc, thoughts of serious diseases and complicated treatments or worse stay on your mind until you find out otherwise. The enemy of our souls tries to manipulate our thinking with thoughts of fear. Joyce Meyers, author of *Battlefield of the Mind*, says that we have to arrest those bad thoughts and replace them with the Word of God.[25] That's what I was thinking when I didn't know what was wrong with me.

Girlfriend Talk

(Gwen) *"I decided I'd better get some supernatural help. I prayed to God for healing. I began to quote scriptures that pertained to healing. I remembered the scripture that said, '...with His stripes we are healed' (Isa. 53:5), and visualized Jesus dying on the cross for my healing. As I thanked Him over and over again, He spoke to me and said, "it was because of this very moment that He decided to die; for that very same healing that would be required that day." He had me in His mind while He suffered bled and died on the cross."*

* * *

When we're dealing with distress, it is a lonely feeling. No matter who is close, when it's all said and done, you are the one suffering through it. It's awesome to know that Christ was thinking of you and me when He stayed on the cross until redemption was complete. Because of His faithfulness we have the promise of healing, deliverance from sin and generational curses, peace of mind and a full life. Fantastic! Think of the self-sacrifice and the love it must have taken for Christ to give His precious life for our benefit so many years in the future. His mind was on us. How about that! We have to see to it that our minds on Him especially during times of trouble. Makes you wanna shout doesn't it! If you are going through sickness or other aliments of life, know that nothing catches God by surprise. He has already prepared for that thing over two thousand years ago. It's like money in the bank. Reach up and receive your deliverance!

> *SISTER TIP: If your sister-friend is sick or has received disturbing news about her health, spend as much time as she will allow connecting. Pray with her and for her. Remind your sisters about the price Christ paid for our healing and help her laugh out loud sometimes. Send a get well card with this poem. I believe it will bring a sense of comfort to her.*

Pray Together:

Heavenly Father, Thank You for sending Your Son to give His life for our salvation and our healing. We don't want to ever take it lightly or forget the provision made for every situation that may arise in our lives. We are so privileged to have Your love. Help us not to be overwhelmed by our troubles but overflow us with Your love. In Jesus' name, Amen.

READ THIS:

But he was wounded for our transgressions, he was bruised for our iniquities: the chastisement of our peace was upon him; and with his stripes we are healed. Isaiah 53:5 (KJV)

DISCUSSION STARTERS:

- Share a time you experienced supernatural healing.

- Tell someone else's story as was told to you.

Notes:

Words of Inspiration:

I'm connected to a powerful agreement
Father, Son, Holy Ghost and me consent
When I agree with the Trinity
It clears a path to victory

Demons fall on every side
My mouth a canon of fire intensified
Spouting out the promises of God
Together we become a bomb squad

Able to conquer Satan's power that be
Able to stop the hand of the enemy
This power, I have is an indescribable force
Gives Satan no other recourse
Than to flee at the mention of Jesus' name
With his lies, his gimmicks,
his plans put to shame

I'm secure in this circle of security
I have the Word of God as my guarantee
I'M CONNECTED!

Connected

People say that it's not what you know but who you know that counts. The world's success thrives on rubbing shoulders with the influential and the powerful people. Sometimes it requires "sucking up," putting your dignity aside to get ahead. Just one phone call from the right party can change events in a person's life forever. Being connected is so special that people take on the importance of those they are connected to. I've found in that the mere mention of an important person's name in a conversation gives the listener and the speaker a sense of importance. Who are you connected with?

Girlfriend Talk

(Gwen) *"My family was homeless. We had been trying to find a place to live for a year at no avail. My friend and co-worker who was connected to the city's commissioner learned about the situation and, with one phone call to the commissioner, made arrangements for us to participate in a transitional program and move into a four-bedroom home within a couple of months. God kept our family together throughout those sensitive times and long after the crisis was over. For three years I saw Him bring peace, love, favor and yes even joy to our family during those troubled times. The program's counselor that was assigned to us was so impressed with our sense of stability that she only made one visit.*

When it was time to leave the program, God gently led us to another four-bedroom home which we rented with no credit check. Interestingly, the program ended as soon as we left. It was as if God had held it together until our stay was completed. God was the one that orchestrated the availability of the home, the timing, the willingness of my friend to get an audience with the commissioner on my behalf. It suited us perfectly as if God had prepared it just for us. "

* * *

If that's what connections will do in this world, imagine being connected to the King of the Universe! Some things only God can do. What a privilege to have Him on our side. You don't have to "suck up;" all you have to do is be obedient to His Word. When you have the favor of King of Kings, what else do you need?

> *SISTER TIP: When we connect ourselves to God we become connected to each other. Show some love. Team up with someone in prayer, in mission, in sharing, in creativity, in anything good, wholesome, and worthy of praise.*

Pray Together:

Dear God, You are awesome. Thank You for sharing Your greatness with us. Lord, we know connecting to people can be scary, even though we have a hard time living without them. Sometimes we forget that Your Word tells us through Jesus Christ we can do all things. As long as we stay connected to You, we will walk discerning the good from the bad. Help us to walk in faith believing Your Word, to stay connected and to help others get connected too. In Jesus' name we pray, Amen.

READ THIS:

Abide in me and I in you. As the branch cannot bear fruit of itself, except it abide in the vine; no more can ye, except ye abide in me. John 15: 5 (KJV)

DISCUSSION STARTERS:

- Describe a time when you needed help from others but you were afraid to ask.

- Describe a time when you would have connected to others but you hadn't developed a friendship strong enough to feel comfortable in.

- Describe a time when you felt especially close to God.

Notes:

Words of Inspiration:

I saw you from afar
the door to your heart ajar
wondering whether to approach or not, shrinking rejection you thought

I could tell you needed me
we're not inseparable like we use to be, some of the old scars were fresh
again some pain rebound again

I saw the old limps I saw you wince
I saw your love lag
Baffled trying to come back

I know the blocks you stumbled over, Swimming upstream to get over
Passage pregnant with pitfalls
I wished you had called

I already know the scope of your fears I taste your tears
Each day I hear your cries and feel your sighs
My heart aches to see you afraid

Don't you know that I haven't given you the spirit of fear?
Don't you know you have the power to persevere?
You weren't meant to walk alone, Not during my boundless throne

I'm enduring, everlasting, never ending, I'm timeless, term less and relentless
Hold on to me, I'll guide you through Remember, you're my child.

I ABSOLUTELY ADORE YOU!

Come to Me

It really feels weird when we think we've messed up our relationship with Jesus. The natural inclination to run the other way in shame can feel like the only way out. But that's a trick of Satan. Jesus is not like some lovers or friends. We don't have to be timid to approach Him even when we have sinned. His love is everlasting. He's always ready to forgive when you ask Him. He doesn't remember your sins anymore. He won't ever bring them back up in your face. (1 John 1:9)

Girlfriend Talk

(Francine) *"I was disappointed and devastated when I finally saw my husband's true self. I thought he would change over time but things got worse. I needed something, someone to listen to me and treat me with love and attention. I didn't go looking for it, but it presented itself through a mutual friend. I was intrigued by how he hung onto my every word, followed my conversations, asked questions and scrolled back to a previous comment to make a connection with a later one. He was listening to me. My conversations with my husband were only on a need-to-know basis.*

For months, my friend and I talked. We were like two lovebirds courting and I totally turned to him to meet my needs. It was thrilling, but I lived a secret life all the while, working in the church. I led the choir but things wouldn't flow. My musical gift wouldn't act right. I could feel Jesus calling me back to Him. He knew all along what was going on. Surprisingly, even though I was dead wrong, I felt His love calling me. Finally after a long time of sneaking around and pretending, I gave up my friendship and ran to God. He never gave up on me. He forgave me as He promised and now I trust Him for my life. My marriage has improved in many ways. It's not perfect, but I put my love for God above anything else. I know He loves me and will take care of me."

* * *

Even though we know better, it's easy to run to the wrong places, people and things to fill a void in our lives, but those decisions eventually cause us to be burdened, scared, worrisome and plain old worn out. Don't wallow in the guilt the devil will try to bring you. Jesus wants us to come to Him. Matthew 11:28 say "Come unto me all ye that labor and are heavy laden and I will give you rest." (KJV)

Admit your faults to Jesus. Go to Him. He is willing and ready to forgive and help you put your life back in order.

Maybe you haven't sinned, but you've gotten a little distant. Spend some personal time with Him; reboot your relationship.

> SISTER TIP: Testify to three sisters in Christ about God's mercy and grace for your life as an encouragement and celebrate! Have a "Welcome Back" celebration for those who have strayed a little. It will encourage them.

Pray Together:

Dear Jesus, Thank You for searching for us with Your heart. It is Your heart that loves us even when we fall short of grace. Thank You for providing a way to confess our sins, our shortcomings and our faults. Please forgive us for trying to make it on our own. Remind us that it is only through Your strength that we can live victorious lives. Thank You for loving us so much. In Jesus' name we pray, Amen.

READ THIS:

Even so it is not the will of the Father which is in heaven that one of these little ones should perish. Matthew 18:14 (KJV)

DISCUSSION STARTERS:

If you do not know Jesus as your personal savior, I can't think of a better time to fill that void. I'm sure your friend(s) won't mind praying along with you now.

Notes:

_____
_____
_____
_____
_____
_____
_____
_____
_____
_____
_____
_____
_____
_____
_____
_____
_____
_____
_____
_____
_____
_____
_____
_____
_____
_____
_____
_____
_____
_____
_____

Dear Jesus,

Thank You for this chance to ask You to come into my life and make me a whole person. I come just like I am; a sinner. I believe You are the son of God and that You died for me. I believe that God raised You from the dead to live within my heart. So God come into my heart and I will live for You. In Jesus' name we pray, Amen.

I know you feel better! Stay connected to people who love and serve God. It gets better from here.

- If you are saved from your sins, describe a time when you've gotten distant and you knew God was wooing you back to Him. How did He do it and how long did it take for you to answer?

WAS IT GOOD FOR YOU, TOO?

Intimate issues are issues of the soul. This section will explore subjects that we may not readily speak openly about but need to be addressed.

Almost every woman yearns to have a Boaz in her life like Ruth in the Bible, who loves and cares for her but many are like Hagar, who found herself a single mother displaced and alone.

It's not always good for everyone, we may have some bumps and bruises to get over but with God and the love of sisters who could relate, we can make it through.

I hope by this time you and your traveling buddies may have become more comfortable talking and sharing with each other. Take a risk. Be honest about your experiences and your feelings.

Note: Through this section you may be called upon to administer more hugs, wipe more tears and rejoice more deeply together. Be liberal.

Words of Inspiration:

I think I'm a strong woman
able to support and stand
hang tough;
bounce back like elastic band,

do my share to carry the load
put my shoulder to the wheel
ignore what I feel:
but sometimes I need arms.

Arms to comfort me, uphold me,
secure me
not
seduce me or suffocate me.

Arms that understand me,
empathize, sympathize
not scrutinize.

Arms that love and keep me
close to the heart,
to protect me from trouble
before it starts
not

to impress me, oppress me or
depress me.

Arms that develop me
from where I am
and envelop me for
who I grow to become,

Arms that lift me up above the
shadows
And answer my questions before I
ask them

Arms that embrace me
Not disgrace me
Rest me
Not stress me
Upgrade me
Not degrade me

Whew! Sometimes I think I need
supernatural arms.

Arms

Girlfriend Talk

Gwen) *"I spent the greater part of my marriage trying to get my husband to behave in the manner in which I wanted him. I wanted a "Bill Cosby" TV personality husband, one that is portrayed on "The Cosby Show",* [26] *one that would anticipate my desires before I could ask for them and never have a problem with almost anything I ask. I wanted a husband who would go to great lengths to make me and the children happy and who would listen to my deepest heartfelt concerns whenever I began to share them. The problem was he wasn't lining up to my measurements. I would get upset and disappointed when he didn't fulfill my "needs." In my mind he obviously didn't understand what he was supposed to do. So I set out to teach him the proper way to be a husband. I used a variety of techniques to help him understand my point of view. Of course, as you may imagine, levels of dissention grew between us. Then one day I heard the Lord say to me, "leave him alone." I was a little insulted but I decided to not say anything else about issues that came up concerning his role as husband. I let it go and turned to God for my needs. When I did, within a week's time (honestly), I was so surprised. My husband came home saying everything I had been telling him as if they were all his ideas. Of course I wanted desperately to point out that I had been saying those same thoughts which he ignored for a long time, but I didn't. I just praised God in my heart."*

* * *

We have a habit of looking to ourselves or expecting someone else to supply our needs. Certain roles we believe husbands and boyfriends, even friends are to play in our lives and sometimes rightfully so.

But what happens when they don't? Do we allow negative emotions to consume us? Do we demand it? It was God who promised to supply ALL of our needs.

Remember? God showed me that He knew my needs no matter how simple they were and He was able and willing to meet them through whatever means He chose. This is where our faith is seen. Do we believe that God will do what He says, even in our relationships? Psalms 138:8a tells us that God will perfect those things that concern us.

Our needs list can be pretty long, but our job is to go to God in prayer and expect Him to meet them. Sometimes what we think we need is not what we really need. God can handle that too.

Decide to take your list to God. Leave it there and trust Him to supply. You know how we get together with our girlfriends and discuss our men? Well, next time try reminding each other that it's God who supplies our needs. Be ready to use your arms to give plenty of hugs, (just a little strength for the wait.) Don't fret, fuss or complain. Only God can change hearts and minds anyway.

SISTER TIP: Find a sister who needs a hug. Get with a bunch of other girlfriends and take a picture of all your arms extended for a big bear hug. Send it to her or a teddy bear with hugging arms. Send this poem and a basket of comforting treats. Better yet give her some real hugs. Hugs are circles of love. I don't think we can get too much good love.

Pray Together:

Lord, sometimes we forget who You are and we get caught up in worrying. Help us to remember that You are all powerful and well able to meet all of our needs; spiritual, physical, intellectual, relational, financial and emotional. Help us to release our control, our timetables, and our agendas in favor of Your guidance. In Jesus' name we pray, Amen.

READ THIS:

And my God will liberally supply (fill to the full) your every need according to His riches in glory in Christ Jesus. Philippians 4:19 (AMPLIFIED BIBLE)

DISCUSSION STARTERS:

- Make a list of people, emotions and things you want God to move on.

- Describe a time when you felt that no one was listening to your needs and you had to see to it that they did?

Notes:

Words of Inspiration:

GET IT IN YOUR HEART
MAKE A START
PREPARE YOUR MIND
TAKE THE TIME
CHANGE YOUR WILL
STIMULATE YOUR SKILL
MANAGE YOUR MOUTH
CHASE AWAY DOUBT
TAKE STOCK
SET THE CLOCK
PRIORTIZE
AIM HIGH
DRAW NIGH
MAGNIFY
SPEND SOME TIME WITH GOD

How to Form a Relationship

Are you fed up with a relationship that's not going anywhere? The other party just won't act right? Let's face it, we're opposites. Even though it makes good sense to us to think a certain way, those same thoughts can be processed completely differently in the minds of our male counterparts. Remember the Mars and Venus concept? So you're not crazy and neither are they. We're just different.

Girls, we want good relationships. We dream about it. We crave it. At all cost sometimes, we work at it. But our methods are not always effective. It's difficult when we do not know the minds and inner workings of others. Before you give up completely, take the emphasis off of the other person for a moment. Practice with God. Spending time with God is the foundation to all good relationships. He'll lead you and show you what to do. If we follow His relationship and communication principles, things will work out better than we can dream. By all means, live your life in the joy of the Lord.

Girlfriend Talk

(KIM) *"I was attracted to Isaiah by his love for God. He satisfied one of the top items on my list for potential husbands. We spent a lot of time on the phone, (he called me almost every night.) We'd talk and pray together each time. I really enjoyed that. He would drive from his home in another state to visit me often and things looked like they were progressing. Could marriage be in the air? As time went on, it became obvious that we didn't share the same beliefs on some issues; important issues. I tried to keep an open mind but when Isaiah went AWOL in my life, it was obvious the relationship was over. I was very hurt. Even though I felt like I had lost the "dream" I wasn't devastated, thanks to God. Having a close relationship with God kept me from compromising my body and heart. I would still be trying to work through the hurt today if my relationship with God wasn't first in my life."*

* * *

Rejection, hurt, misunderstandings are some side effects of relationships that can make you want to give up on them altogether. Forming a relationship with God is the easiest one to have. God *desires* to be with you and He meets us most of the way. He promised never to turn his back on us. You can't get better than that. How well do you know God? Our finite minds could never know everything about Him but He knows us better than we know ourselves. As we spend more time with open hearts getting to know Him, we'll understand ourselves better. That's half the battle in your other relationships.

Reflect on your relationship with God. Be determined to know Him better. It will take a little work, so expect it. God will teach you how to handle your other relationships; He'll protect you from and through the toxic ones. Better yet, He'll help orchestrate them all if you let Him. He's that into you.

> *SISTER TIP: For one week, get to know a sister in Christ by talking and spending time together in godly companionship. Bless her with something that means a lot to her. This could be the beginning of a great friendship.*

Pray Together:

Lord, we want to get to know You better. We want to commune with You like Adam did in the Garden of Eden. Help us to do what it takes to spend quality time loving You. Keep our hearts open to receive Your Word. Thank You for wanting to be close to us. Lord help us not to get caught up in our own emotions that we go ahead of You and make bad choices. Lead and teach us how to have healthy relationships with others in Your will for us. For those of us that are still waiting, help us not to become anxious but to remember that in Your time it will come to past. In Jesus' name we pray, Amen.

READ THIS:

My heart is fixed, O God, my heart is steadfast and confident! I will sing and make melody. Awake my glory (my inner self); awake, harp and lyre! I will awake right early (I will awaken the dawn.) Psalms 57:7,8 (AMPLIFIED BIBLE)

DISCUSSION STARTERS:

- Describe a time when you felt like your relationship with God was great. What part did you play in making it good?

- How has God orchestrated a relationship or friendship that you are blessed by?

- Describe a time you might have built a relationship that ended in disaster.

Notes:

Words of Inspiration:

Wandering hearts along a road
out of bounds
Who left the gate open? who let them out?
Straggling into other people's yards
Rummaging for a niche
Sucking up artificial light

Wandering hearts lost their way
Hungry for greener grass on the other side
Stalked by fear; love displaced

Nipping on someone else's
table scraps off the floor
Drinking from someone else's
spigot at the back door

Wandering hearts; bathing in guilt
heaping up iniquity; alternate destiny
Look at the house the devil built

dilapidated and leaning
on infidelity's sinking sand
Put in a storm
ready to fall
"AND GREAT WAS THE FALL OF IT"

Wandering hearts
tailspin on a collision course
Crashing into
the supplier of needs
who sees and knows
this make up of hearts
Quick to heal and easy to forgive

Wandering Hearts

We are accustomed to seeing men's eyes wander into the direction of other beautiful women. For men, the sense of vision is very sensitive. Sexually, men are usually stimulated by what they see first. For women, our hearts are very sensitive. We're usually stimulated by how we're treated first. When it comes to infidelity, our hearts wander off long before we wander into someone's arms. Looking for love in all the wrong places leaves us empty and guilt-ridden. The devil whispers to us that having another man would be better than loving the one we have. We feel like the other guy would treat us better or have more money to take better care of us or they may even look better. But the devil tells lies!

If you're single, the same thing can happen. God is your husband. Who can love you and care for you better than God?

Girlfriend Talk

(Asia) *"By the time I realized I was in love it was a year and a husband too late. He treated me like I had always dreamed- like a queen. My husband wasn't like him. I knew it was wrong but I couldn't get him out of my heart. He didn't seem to mind that I was married; he wanted to keep seeing me. He had money and he was fine looking. He would always show up in stores and other places I was in, slipping me gifts and money, telling me what a better life he would give me. It was so tempting and for a while I was reeled into his charm.*

God loved me so much He sent a minister to tell me what I was heading for if I continued down that path. I had to let him go or else nothing in my life would work. It was affecting everything including my ministry. I decided to fall in love with God deeply instead. As I did, the hold was broken, I could walk away. Afterwards I found out that the man was a big time drug dealer. Many times while I was with him, he would make drug runs. I had no idea. It was only the grace of God that kept me safe and out of jail. If I had left my husband for him, I would have been in trouble."

* * *

When our emotions lead us into actions that go against the Word of God, we are walking in the flesh. Paul said in the Bible that in the flesh there lives no good thing, Romans 7:18 (my paraphrase). It's tough searching for help and not knowing where to find it. So let me cut your search short. I'm sure you have valid needs but Jesus is the only answer. He will lead and guide you into the truth. He will help you to go through the difficult times as you wait on your deliverance - and He will deliver you.

Girlfriend Talk

(Kim) *I thought sleeping with the right guy would fulfill me; but after, I felt the same way every time. It didn't matter how fine he was or how good he was in bed. I couldn't shake the incredible empty feeling I was left with."*

> SISTER TIP: *Know a sister with heart trouble? Get some reinforcements. Grab a sister in the Lord. Turn up the heat on the devil. Keep your heart on Jesus and His work. You are going to make it. God loves and forgives.*

Pray Together:

Lord Thank You for Your incredible mercy and Your untiring grace. When we feel our hearts wandering off into places that are not good for us to go- especially when our hearts are broken and hurting from past relationships, help us to recognize that our feelings of emptiness and loneliness are indications of our hearts yearning for You. We trust You for complete deliverance and direction. Remind us to fill our hearts with Your Word. Lord when we've gotten off the right track, forgive us and direct our paths away from the guilt and shame. Direct us back to You. In Jesus' name we pray, Amen.

READ THIS:

But I say, walk and live habitually in the (Holy) Spirit (responsive to and controlled and guided by the Spirit); then you will certainly not gratify the cravings of the flesh (of human nature without God) Galatians 5:16 (AMPLIFIED BIBLE)

DISCUSSION STARTERS:

- Have you ever fantasized how it would be to make love to someone else besides the man you are married to?

- Do you find yourself engrossed in romance novels or sentimental love songs as a substitute for the real thing?

- Are you in a relationship where there's a lack of affection?

Notes:

Words of Inspiration:

It was God's idea
when He created a man and a woman to enjoy the fruit of the body
and indulge in pleasure beyond compare

It was God's idea to design a man
with a firm life shuttle and a rhythm that makes your toes flare

It was God's idea
to provide a passageway in a woman where life could travel
and produce a son and heir

It was God's idea
to create the libido as a locomotive that blends the two together
in a heated love affair

The gift that God gave husband and wife is life long and undefiled
holy, versatile never out of style

Only God could create such pleasure in bed
that would make your eyes roll to the back of your head

Lust, on the other hand
is the devil's version of God's intimacy doing it his way
makes the whole plan go off key

It was God's creation
so He gets to make the rules the directions of the gift
and how it must be used

God made the woman for the man but we don't belong to every
Rick, Charlie and Chan

We're precious and set aside for that particular one

Who demonstrates his love in a marital sum

So unwrap your gift my married sister don't be shy
enjoy heaven's blessing
just make sure that man "QUALIFIES"

Special Gift

I almost decided not to include this poem in the book for fear that my words would be too blunt and would offend some readers. But then, I remembered that sex is the special gift that God created for our pleasure and procreation. The enemy of our souls has perverted it and has made it taboo to discuss even in a correct manner in our adult Christian circles. It's not the one sinful thing God lets Christians do, as I have heard it said; it's another example of His grace and mercy towards us. It's time we set the record straight.

There are several benefits to God's gift of sex. It relieves stress and exercises the body which in turn stimulates sleep. It relieves pent up passions and creates closeness between husband and wife. If it brings babies to the family, that also reminds us of how great God must be to create such a powerful expression of love. It's a privilege to have this gift available to us.

Sexual intimacy is totally giving yourself to the person you love; no holding back, being completely available and deeply communicating your love to each other.

Sometimes women complain that sex is all the husbands ever think about (and they do think about it a lot, I agree). But consider this: it is by divine design that he is created to be the loving leader of the couple.

Now don't get me wrong, I'm not saying that he is the one that should initiate sex every time, but that his physical make-up encourages sex often.

Girlfriend Talk

(Gwen) *"I used to think my husband was selfish and immature because of how often he would ask for sex. It didn't seem to matter what was going on; when he was focused, he was focused. I soon found out that most married women had the same feelings. That sent me searching for answers and I learned that men are wired that way; that the hormone testosterone creates a sexual urge in their brains every 12 to 15 minutes! Afterwards, I not only began to understand his drive but to pray for him as he battled the forces of nature and the enemy's manipulation in the world.*

Even though I may not be driven as often as he is, I've decided to be more available for him to express his love and passion to me. I thank God for the commitment he renews to me and God on a daily basis."

* * *

Think of the benefits we would lose if he wasn't very interested. Count your blessings, girl! That man wants to love *your* body. God instructs us not to allow things to come between these special times together, (1 Corinthians 7:2-4.) Don't allow the devil to cheat you out of this awesome gift. It is a proven fact that the best sexual experiences are enjoyed by married couples. Every time you and our husband engage in sex, you bring praises to the one who created it. He could have made it instinctive only, but He designed it for your pleasure as well. Like any gift from God, He wants us to fully enjoy it. So plan a special night (or morning or afternoon) to blow that man's mind. Nobody can do it like a wife!

> SISTER TIP: Get some tips from some church mothers who are seasoned in the Lord or if they are not available read: Red-Hot Monogamy: Making Your Marriage Sizzle by Bill and Pam Farrel.[27]

If you are single, what an opportunity you have to give yourself exclusively to God. Make an evening of it! Sing, pray, listen to his wonderful voice and be refreshed. Remember it's about deep intimacy. If you open your heart I guarantee He'll blow your mind every time.

For those of you who have recently become single or your husbands have succumbed to the temptation of being unfaithful, there is nothing quite as hurtful. My prayer for you is that God will take you through this time, insulate your heart with His love and wrap you in His arms of comfort.

Pray Together:

Lord, Thank You for the gift of intimacy. You could have made us like the animals instinctively engaging in the act. But you've made us like Yourself, experiencing depths and heights of sacred love. Help us to stay close to each other. Keep our marriages strong. Thank You for the ability and freedom to express guiltless passion to the ones we gave our lives to. In Jesus' name we pray, Amen.

READ THIS:

Let him kiss me with the kisses of his mouth; for thy love is better than wine. Song of Solomon 1:2(KJV)

DISCUSSION STARTERS:

- It is said that the sexual orgasm is a glimpse of the intensity of God's love for us. Describe a time when your lovemaking session with your husband reminded you of a worship time with God.

- Describe a time when you needed the grace of God's presence during love making.

- As a single woman, describe any sensual adjustments you've made to invite God into that intimate place in your heart.

Notes:

Words of Inspiration:

Way down deep in
the middle of the soul
sits a well filled
with the desires of a heart
waiting to be satisfied
brick on top of brick
a hollowed wall
around them

formed by dreams,
visions and experiences
precious, volatile
yearning

standing desires
afraid to be stirred
future disappointment
brought into the present
some days leaking

what if he don't..?
what if it doesn't..?
what if....

secret desires
dark with trapped hurt
unspoken dreams some days seepin

if only he could be...
if only I could do...
if only...

Why don't you dare?
let Christ in
and give up the title
"keeper of the key"
Your desires are vaulted with Him
They're already known by Him
could only be done well through
Him

Priority
get delighted in Him
and your desires?
As good as got.

The Desires of a Heart

Nobody knows the heart like Jesus. People say one thing but mean something else. Who could know? I've hesitated to allow others to know my deepest desires or even verbalize them to myself because I couldn't stand to be hurt if they didn't come true.

If you're single, longing for a mate is a common desire, not just for sex (even though that's important too!), but also for someone with whom you can share the good and bad things; someone to love you and be there for the little things. Our heart's desires can be so passionate, that we guard them with all of our might and we are sometimes consumed by them. I learned that Jesus promised to give us those desires after we give ourselves totally to Him.

I believe our desires have to go through a cleansing process. Our motives may not be right, our intentions may be warped, and our reasoning could be affected by past hurts. As things change in our lives, our desires may even change.

Girlfriend Talk

(Shannon) *"I was so in love with Sean, I was seeing his initials everywhere: on billboards, in books, in my phone and in my dreams. Now the dreams had me going because many times God talks to me in dreams. My heart wanted to believe that Sean was for me and all I could think about was that. Even though he wasn't saved, I felt like God would save him for me. I knew I loved God enough that I wouldn't compromise my testimony but I really wanted to see this desire come to pass. I began manipulating and setting up ways for it to happen. All along I was hearing the quiet voice of God saying leave it alone. My mom told me to leave it alone, and my girlfriend told me to leave it alone, but I needed to see him and feel it for myself. I got my opportunity.*

On one of his trips to my town, we arranged a meeting. As soon as I saw him, I had a very strong direction from God saying, 'LEAVE IT ALONE.' I knew what I had to do and God gave me the strength to do it. I left it alone. I gave the subject of Sean to the Lord. If God wanted me to hook up with Sean, He would have to do it. I still have the desire to be with him and I still have dreams sometimes, but God is first. He has the power to change things, but I only want what God wants for me. I know that He knows best."

* * *

Only God knows the future of our destinies. He will give us what we need, things that will enhance us and not destroy us. Don't think He isn't concerned about your needs. God knows your heart. It is His will that we live abundant lives. Today, choose to give your desires to God. Give him the key to your heart- all of your heart. Trust Him to keep your desires and place them in the proper time.

SISTER TIP: Speaking the desires of your heart in faith is another way of trusting God for them. Share some of your heart desires with a trusted sister in the Lord and believe God together for them. Double up and make one of those joining paper hearts, write some of your desires and corresponding scriptures on them and switch. Each team prays for the hearts.

Pray Together:

Lord, Thank You for loving us so much that You would think to make provisions for our hearts. Lord, help us not to allow our desires to become our lord. Cleanse our motives and our intentions so they come from a pure heart to worship You. Guide our patience as we learn to trust You with these precious, precious desires. In Jesus' name we pray, Amen.

READ THIS:

Delight yourself also in the Lord and He will give you the desires and secret petitions of your heart. Psalms 37:4 (AMPLIFIED BIBLE)

DISCUSSION STARTERS:

Discuss a time when your deepest desires conflicted with God's will, and knowing it didn't stop you from wanting it. What did you do?

Testify of a time when God gave you a desire of your heart.

Notes:

Words of Inspiration:

Inside a rut
a weary habit works
to rent a place for
faulty understanding
and misdirected passions.
In Lo Debar
Broken down reasoning forgets that
what is felt is different
from what is real.
insight smogged up by leftover dreams
and second hand excitement.
Hope near empty at times.

The place situates itself within
the center of wealth for
Renewed Minds Only
where the soil is rich with the power of
prayer
and fertilization is the Word of God.
Truth reaches out to callings and destiny
"opened doors" and "ways made" are
funded by faith
Love makes ability soar
and imagination squeaks
only in the presence of miracles.
Citizenship is encouraged but not imposed,
you have to want it.

Awake! oh zion
put on your strength!
Shake yourself from the dust girl!
Arise!
Shake yourself from the dust!
you have to want it.

Inside a Rut

There are times when we're in a seductive little hole of sameness that lures us into a semblance of comfort. Unfortunately that comfortable spot can lead into depression, weariness, and boredom, making it difficult to defeat. The rut can occur in every phase of life and it creeps in slowly.

Let's investigate and determine if things have been the same for an extended period of time. Are you blaming others for your bored life? Are you just going through the motions at church? Has your hairstyle been the same for ten years? Do you find yourself avoiding your scheduled Tuesday night love-making session at 7:30 p.m. sharp (married ladies only)? If the answer is yes, yes, yes, the question is why, why, why?

Girlfriend Talk

(Joanne) *"I found myself in a rut after my daughter grew up and left home. I guess I got used to being alone. I didn't really notice it until my girlfriend came over and tried to get me to go out for a walk or something. With her at my house, I'm very uncomfortable. I had gotten used to staying in my room alone. I even stopped putting Christmas decorations out at holiday time."*

(Gwen) *"You just get caught up in the day to day routines. You forget it's been a long time since something exciting has happened in your life. You settle in. But eventually, it feels heavy. I decided to color my hair to make a change in me. It really perked things up in the marriage. It was like I had gotten ten years younger."*

* * *

Once we discover where we are, something has to be done. If you really pay attention to the words used in the scripture, you'll notice that we are the ones that are instructed to make the changes. "People who allow themselves to be passive have a type of deadness inside them that is frightening. Their get-up-and-go has gotten up and gone."[28] Take the responsibility. Jesus wants us to have abundant life (John 10:10), nothing less. God says to sing a new song to Him. That means do something that you normally don't do.

Surprise your honey with a love-making session on Monday night instead. Change the scenery, wear something silky and see through, play some romantic music. Don't wait for him to do it. Believe me, he'll catch on. Get a new hairstyle: take a class, learn something new. Cook a new dish. If you don't like your figure, you can change that too.

God is a creative and colorful being. Just take a look at the world. Break out! Don't allow satan to talk you into believing that you have to be boring to love God or you're too old to have a good time. Start living in faith. Bump up your devotion time. Really make God Lord over your life. The rest will be easier to change.

If you are single do as Ruth did in the Bible. Be holy and be accessible to those godly Boaz(es).

Walk out of whatever has you bound and walk into your divine destiny. Go ahead, make some changes. I hope you want to.

Pray Together:

Lord, we don't always know when we fall into a rut but we're thankful that we can call on You to help pull us out. Thank You for showing it up through our friends, our family, our mirrors, or even through our frustrations. We know that the rut can be a vehicle of bondage filled with fear, regret, and dread. The enemy can use it to bind us. But You are our salvation. Help us to break out, bust loose. We look to You to lead us and guide us as we make changes that will glorify You. In Jesus' name we pray, Amen.

READ THIS:

And He has put a new song in my mouth, a song of praise to our God. Many shall see and fear (revere and worship) and put their trust and confident reliance in the Lord. Psalms 40:3 (AMPLIFIED BIBLE)

DISCUSSION STARTERS:

Describe a time when you've been in a spiritual rut but were or weren't aware of it.

Describe having your love life in a rut. What got you out and how long did it take?

Describe when you were in a personal rut. When and what changes did you make?

Notes:

Words of Inspiration:

To my Beloved, You're so beautiful, my darling so beautiful, and your dove eyes are veiled by your hair as it flows and shimmers, like a flock of goats in the distance streaming across a hillside in the sunshine.

Your smile is generous and full— expensive and strong and clean Your lips are jewel red, Your mouth elegant and inviting Your veiled cheeks soft and radiant, The smooth, lithe lines of your neck command notice-all heads turn in awe and admiration! Your breasts are like fawns twins of a gazelle, grazing among the first spring flowers.

The sweet, fragrant curves of your body, the soft, spiced contours of your flesh invite me, and I come. I stay until dawn breathes its light and night slips away You're beautiful from head to toe, my dear love. beautiful beyond compare, absolutely flawless. Come with me from Lebanon, my bride Leave Lebanon behind, and come. Leave your high mountain hideaway. Abandon your wilderness seclusion. Where you keep company with lions and panthers guard your safety. You've captured my heart, dear friend. You looked at me and I fell in love.

One look my way and I was hopelessly in love! How beautiful your love, dear, dear friend- far more pleasing than a fine, rare wine, your fragrance more exotic than select spices. The kisses of your lips are honey, my love, every syllable you speak a delicacy to savor, Your clothes smell like the fresh outdoors, the ozone scent of high mountains.

Dear lover and friend, You're a secret garden, a private and pure fountain. Body and soul, you are paradise, a whole orchard of succulent fruits Ripe apricots and peaches, oranges and pears; nut trees and cinnamon, and all scented woods; mint and lavender, and all herbs aromatic. A garden fountain, sparkling and splashing, fed by spring waters from the Lebanon mountains.

Lovingly, Jesus.

Taken from Song of Solomon 4:1-15 Message Bible

Love Letter

Girlfriend Talk

Renee) *"I received a love letter from a guy when I was in college. It was sort of bittersweet because in the letter, he told me he would have to break off our relationship. He didn't think he could stay faithful to me while he was away. He knew that I loved God and he wasn't into the 'church thing.' It was the sweetest thing. Even though he broke it off, I felt sure of his love for me. I kept it for a very long time."*

(Gwen) *"When my husband wanted to marry me, my grandmother insisted he write letters to all of my parents and guardians asking for my hand in marriage."*

* * *

Within today's technology, cell phones and internet, the art of letter writing is all but dead. There was something about a letter that spelled respect. It required a man to think about and spend time working on how he would approach the woman of his interest. Women still want to be swept off their feet. We want to be the object of a good man's love, his passion and his preoccupation. Well, in this allegory of Christ's love to the Church, the Lord has written such letters. What's so wonderful about these letters is that every word of it is truth. There's no playing, no kidding, no finger crossing behind His back, no rap. God means just what He says. He knows what a girl needs to hear. He knows how to speak to a lady just like she wants to hear it. In the confines of marriage this sensual talk is beautiful and appropriate.

Know who you are. The Bible says we are the glory of the man, 1 Corinthians 11:8b (my paraphrase). The enemy has perverted our thinking to believe that we need to appeal to a man's loins to receive his love. But lust never turns to love. We become a play thing used only for selfish satisfaction. At times we crave a man's love so much that we'll accept being tolerated instead of being celebrated. That's not what our souls want. We're more than a pair of breasts and legs. We're royalty, beauty and grace packaged in destiny. We must carry ourselves as such and insist that we are treated that way.

A man shows his true love by commitment, and you can count on God. It's so good to know that even though He is everything to everyone, you could still have Him all to yourself. He's the sensitive kind. Today, read a love letter to yourself from the Lord. Better yet why don't you send it through the mail to yourself. It may come just when you need it most.

> *SISTER TIP: Be a sister in Christ and send one to another sister who may be feeling a bit alone. Remind her of who she is in Christ.*

Pray Together:

God, how can we count the ways we love You? Thank You for sharing Your love, knowing just what to say at the right time. Your words are life to us. You are our comforter. Show us how to love others as You love us. In Jesus' name, Amen

READ THIS:

For this is the covenant that I will make with the house of Israel after those days, says the Lord; I will put My laws in their mind and write them on their hearts; and I will be their God, and they shall be My people. Hebrews 8:10 (NKJV)

DISCUSSION STARTERS:

- Tell about any love letters you've received.

- Some women say they're excited by the "bad boy" kind of guy. Describe a time when you've fallen for a guy that treated you less respectfully than you wanted.

- What other scriptures are like love letters to you?

Notes:

RETREAT

This is the final lap of the journey, in some ways maybe the most fun.

Start off with the music and snacks suggestions to create the ambience as you further connect your hearts. They are only suggestions. Together, feel free to create your own.

As you read the prayers of the author, no doubt there will be sentiments that you can relate to. Soak them in let them take you to your own experiences.

By now you should have become comfortable with meeting and speaking to each other. You know who is the most like you and who speaks your language, and you have learned from those who are different from you, as well.

I'm sure you might have received insight about yourself and your traveling buddies that have added items to your personal prayer list. Now all of you deserve to relax.

This section provides opportunity to continue learning and enjoying each other's company but it also allows for some deep personal reflection. Don't be afraid to go there. The better you know yourself, the better friend you can be to others.

Write your prayers and listen to what God has to say to you. You may choose to share these things or keep them in your heart. Either way, be blessed.

Day 33 Create an atmosphere

MUSIC: "What A Wonder You Are" A Piece Of My Passion by Juanita Bynum, © 2006 Flow Records TREATS: Strawberry Cheese Cake

Renew

Dear God,

As soon as I kneel down to pray, I hear you say. "RENEW," that's all, but so much comes from that word.

Renew my ailing sense of worth that I seem to be losing with every battle I face.

Renew my health that worries me even though You've promised me healing over and over.

Renew my faith in Your promises for my future that seems to grow foggy as days, weeks and years roll by me.

Renew my ability to stand up for You with the spiritual tenacity that I miss having.

Renew my sense of individuality designed by Your distinct pleasure. Renew the pathway to my destiny that seems to get lost in the crossroads.

Thank You God for loving me so much. You knew I needed it right about now, didn't You? You knew.

Today I receive my renewal through Your Spirit and through Your Word. I know it is a process as well as an immediate change, because when

You speak, things begin to happen. In the spirit world it is already done. By faith, I'll wait until I physically see my change come. Amen.

Dear Child,

But those who wait for the Lord (who expect, look for, and hope in Him) shall change and renew their strength and power; they shall lift their wings and mount up (close to God) as eagles (mount up to the sun); they shall walk and not faint or become tired. Isaiah 40:31(AMPLIFIED BIBLE)

Come to Me, all you who labor and are heavy laden, and I will give you rest. Take My yoke upon you and learn from Me, for I am gentle and lowly in heart, and you will find rest for your souls. Matthew 11: 28- 29 (NKJV)

DISCUSSION STARTER:

- What do you feel about needing renewal?

- What areas do you most often need God to renew in you?

- How do you tell the all powerful God that you are about to blow a fuse or about to demonstrate some other less than Christian virtue?

Notes:

WRITE YOUR OWN PRAYER OF RENEWAL

_____
_____
_____
_____
_____
_____
_____
_____
_____
_____
_____
_____
_____
_____
_____
_____
_____
_____
_____

Waiting for an answer...

What did God say? Write it down.

Day 34 Create an Atmosphere

MUSIC: Hillsong, "Desert Song" This Is Our God; published 2008 by Hillsong Music Australia

TREATS: Ice Cream always goes well with complaining, whatever your flavor of choice.

Crooked Paths

Dear God,

Lord, things are so weird, nothing really earth shattering, just little irritating situations that make my life feel all up hill.

God, I'm just tired; I'm tired of wishing things would settle down and become normal. These problems that are not big enough for an all out battle, yet not small enough to ignore. They are like the beginning of a toothache. The roads I'm on have lots of twists and turns. Complaining has become my psalms. I want to find other roads but I think I'm too worn out. As people say, "my get up and go, got up and went."

Right in the middle of my problem, You sent a sister in Christ to me for help with a much bigger problem. (That's so like You.) How could I help her? I wished someone would help me. But like remote control, the Holy Spirit clicked in. I heard myself ministering to her, reminding her of scriptures and promises that You have promised us in Your Word.

I'm feeling strength coming to my own weary soul as You tell me what to say to her; I'm surprised with the outcome. With my faith revived, You remind me in your Word that You would make my crooked paths straight. Have faith. I believe You because You've never lied to me before. You can't; Your promises are real. Once again You gave me the strength to overcome and go on further. Thank You Lord. Amen.

Dear Child,

I will go before you and level the mountains (to make the crooked places straight); I will break in pieces the doors of bronze and cut asunder the bars of iron. I will give you the treasures of darkness and hidden places that you may know that it is I the Lord, the God of Israel, who calls you by name. Isaiah 45:2-3 (AMPLIFIED BIBLE)

And the ransomed of the Lord shall return, And come to Zion with singing, With everlasting joy on their heads. They shall obtain joy and gladness, and sorrow and sighing shall flee away. Isaiah 35:10 (NKJV)

DISCUSSION STARTER:

- Is it wrong to complain?

- How often do you find yourself complaining?

- What kinds of things bring it on?

Notes:

WRITE YOUR OWN PRAYER OF CROOKED PATH

_____
_____
_____
_____
_____
_____
_____
_____
_____
_____
_____
_____
_____
_____
_____
_____
_____
_____
_____

Waiting for an answer...

What did God say? Write it down.

Day 35 Create an Atmosphere

MUSIC: I'm Healed; Right Now Praise by Jonathon Nelson ©2008 Integrity Media Inc.

TREATS: Fruit Salad is a healthy snack.

He Restores My Soul

Dear Lord,

You know, God, You're beautiful. When I least expect it, sometimes even at the end of the day when I'm just saying goodnight to You, there You are giving direction to my life, bringing light to my path, whispering secrets right into my heart. When I least expect it, You're working things through for me, answering my prayers, bringing rest, leading me to still waters. When I least expect it, there You are delivering, restoring my soul. Amen.

Dear Child,

I will restore to you the years that the locust hath eaten, the cankerworm, and the caterpillar, and the palmerworm. Joel 2:25a (KJV)

The Lord will guide you continually, satisfy your soul in drought, and strengthen your bones; You shall be like a watered garden, And like a spring of water, whose waters do not fail. Isaiah 58:11 (NKJV)

DISCUSSION STARTER:

- Tell about an incident when God surprised you when it looked like you were at your wits' end.

- Talk about times when you may have needed to be restored but it took a while to recognize the restoration.

- What about a time when you didn't think you needed anything until God began to minister to you?

Notes:

_____

_____

_____

_____

_____

_____

_____

_____

_____

_____

_____

_____

_____

_____

_____

_____

_____

_____

_____

_____

_____

_____

_____

_____

_____

_____

_____

_____

WRITE YOUR OWN PRAYER OF RESTORATION

_____
_____
_____
_____
_____
_____
_____
_____
_____
_____
_____
_____
_____
_____
_____
_____

Waiting for an answer...

What did God say? Write it down.

Day 36 Create an Atmosphere

MUSIC: This song expresses relationship we have with God. It's been sweeping the nation, "Never Would've Made It" Thirsty by Marvin Sap Zomba Recording LLC published 2007

TREATS: Oreo Cookie Milk Shakes are wonderful. Loving conversations are easy with milk shakes.

The Vial

Dear Lord,

As I pray this morning, I am aware that you are storing my prayers like a lover keeps old love letters in protection. I'm awed at the thought that You would deem my prayers as precious. I feel so loved. Dear God, You are awesome. Your love is awesome. No one could love me like You. In Revelations, the last book of the Bible, John, the writer tells about a vial You hold in your hand that contained the prayers of the saints.

To think that my prayers are not just being heard but they're being kept makes me more careful of what I say to You. Like a lover writes love letters to her love, she is careful that she speaks words from her heart. She is careful not to waste the precious moments she has. I want our time together to be good quality time. I want to prepare for our special talks. I want my mind to be clear and open to receive from You. I want to sing to You, wait for You, take notice of Your workings in my life, tell You how much I love You, and tell You my deepest secrets. I want to praise You for who You are and to ask You for blessings for others because You are so capable to do that. I want to thank You for everything. Amen.

Dear Child,

Call unto me and I will answer thee and shew thee great and mighty things which thou knowest not. Jeremiah 33.3 (KJV)

And it shall come to pass that before (you) call, I will answer and while (you) are yet speaking, I will hear. Isaiah 65:24 (KJV)

DISCUSSION STARTER:

Tell about a time you realized that God was like a lover to you.

Discuss a time when you needed a "hug" from God.

Talk about your attitude of prayer. Are there any preparations you do in getting ready for prayer?

Notes:

WRITE YOUR OWN PRAYER EXPRESSING YOuR LOVE RELATIONSHIP WITH GOD

_____
_____
_____
_____
_____
_____
_____
_____
_____
_____
_____
_____
_____
_____
_____

Waiting for an answer...

What did God say? Write it down.

Day 37 Create an Atmosphere

MUSIC: This song by Martha Munizzi has been especially uplifting for me. "I Know The Plans" on The Best Is Yet To Come CD Martha Munizzi Music ©2003

TREATS: Warm Peach and Blueberry Cobbler with coffee or herbal tea sounds like it would go well with the thought of security brought on by commitment. Enjoy!

His Mind Is Full Of Me

Dear Lord,

As I prayed today, You let me know that You are thinking about me. As I go through the days in my life, my situations, and my concerns, You let me know that You are traveling along with me. You are fully aware of what is important to me. You know how I feel about the issues of my days, my family, my money, my life, and my relationships. I'm not alone.

Sometimes, little circumstances gives me a lonely feeling. I feel like I'm on my own and I have to fend for myself. But in every situation of my life: my shortcomings, my fears, my feelings, my phobias, my failures, my successes, my joys, my sadness, my credit, my shame and areas too numerous and complicated to talk about, You're there with me, never leaving me alone, sharing in my life. Thank you, Lord.

I think about an old song that I use to hear the church mothers singing when I was a little girl. It talks about You, God never leaving us. That means a lot.

"I see the lightning flashing I hear the thunder roll I've felt sin's breakers dashing trying to conquer my soul I heard the voice of my Savior telling me still to fight on He promised never to leave me never to leave me alone No, never alone No, never alone He promised never to leave me never to leave me alone."[29]

Thank You, Lord, for thinking of me. Amen.

Dear Child,

For I know the thoughts and plans that I have for you, says the Lord, thoughts and plans for welfare and peace and not for evil, to give you hope in your final outcome. Jeremiah 29:11 (AMPLIFIED BIBLE)

Meditate within your heart... and be still. Offer the sacrifices of righteousness, And put your trust in the Lord. Psalms 4:4-5 (NKJV

DISCUSSION STARTER:

Tell about a time when you discovered that God was thinking about you on an everyday basis?

I heard someone say that God woke him early each morning to pray because after watching him sleep all night He couldn't wait to commune with him. How does it make you feel to imagine Him wanting so much to spend time with you?

Notes:

WRITE YOUR OWN PRAYER OF GOD'S COMMITMENT TO YOU

_____
_____
_____
_____
_____
_____
_____
_____
_____
_____
_____
_____
_____
_____
_____
_____
_____
_____
_____

Waiting for an answer...

What did God say? Write it down.

Day 38 Create an Atmosphere

MUSIC: Crystal Lewis Beauty for Ashes; Beauty for Ashes; Metro 1 Music published 1996

TREATS: Chocolate covered strawberries is a treat fitting for an afternoon or evening realization of how much we're loved.

Take a Deep Breath

Dear God,

As I kneel down to prayer, my palms sweaty and my chest filled with stress, I come to You in a terrible way. Tension fills me like a balloon as water fills a bottle, heavy, ready to fall and bust; I do fall. I fall on my knees, no one else to turn to but You. I can feel that You have time to wait until I can speak words. You have time to hear me out.

All I managed was groans at first. Thank You. I talk about everything even before I properly address You as I've been taught. I apologize, feeling that You will accept it urging me to go on. I do, releasing anger, complaining, describing my hurts, explaining why things are too hard for me to deal with, and asking for relief. I feel Your love and understanding.

My kneeling position had long changed to a sitting/lying down position comfortable in your presence- my heart still breaking - out of words again.

I hear You say, "Take a deep breath," I do. I remember that You had told me that once before. A flood of tears flows out with the third exhalation, washing the anger, hurt and stress away. I feel lighter, praising You - marveling at how good I feel - feeling stronger inside - taking a few more deep breaths. Then right in the middle of my praise, I hear You say, "Get your war clothes on. I've given you the power to run through troops and leap over walls." Amen.

Dear Child,

Then shall ye call upon me, and ye shall go and pray unto me and I will hearken unto you, and ye shall seek me, and find me, when ye shall search for me with all your heart. Jeremiah 29: 12, 13 KJV

When wisdom enters your heart, And knowledge is pleasant to your soul, Discretion will preserve you, Understanding will keep you, To deliver you from the way of evil. Proverbs 2:10-11

DISCUSSION STARTER:

- Tell about a time when you sensed God's understanding heart during a circumstance when you may not have been right.

- Have you ever felt overwhelmed with life, but God didn't release you from what He had called you to do?

Notes:

WRITE YOUR OWN PRAYER OF GOD'S UNDERSTANDING

Waiting for an answer...

What did God say? Write it down.

Day 39 Create an Atmosphere

MUSIC: Joe Pace; "When I Worship" Worship for the Kingdom Released October 23, 2007 ©2007 EMI Gospel/ Alliant

Treats: Walnut Brownies with Vanilla Ice Cream

Narrow Places

Dear Lord,

You've said in Your Word that You would lead us into all truth. Lord, I seem to be in a time when all of my dreams are at a standstill as if my destiny is on hold. I would be in a rut except I am aware that things are standing still and I am doing all I can to change it. I get frustrated pushing against brick walls. When I try to make big changes, I feel like I'm spinning until my head hits the ceiling and I come crashing down. Well Lord, who wants to keep doing that?

In my prayer time, it seemed like I wasn't getting any answers. But then You sent the answer through one of Your ministers who told me that life situations had put me in a narrow place. You showed me through Your Word that during these times I must stand still, trust You and hold on because You will bring me out. You always give me a way of escape. You will sustain me with Your strength and You will never leave me.

You instructed me to make small moves, do things I could manage. Save the grandiose projects for later and wait on Your guidance. Then, You comforted me when You showed me that You can still use me to do great things for Your kingdom, even now.

It is during these times that You have my greatest attention. It is during these times that I rely on You the most. It is during these times that I realize just how insufficient I am and how great You are. There is only enough room in this narrow place to turn to You. Amen.

Dear Child,

To everything there is a season, A time for every purpose under heaven:… A time to plant, And a time to pluck what is planted;… A time to break down, And a time to build up; A time to weep, And a time to laugh; …Ecclesiastes 3:1-4 (NKJV)

Now unto him who is able to keep you without stumbling or slipping or falling, and to present you unblemished (blameless and faultless) before the presence of his glory in triumphant joy and exultation (with unspeakable ecstatic delight). (AMPLIFIED BIBLE) Jude 24

Being confident of this very thing, that He who begun a good work in you will complete it until the day of Jesus Christ. Philippians 1:3 NJKV

DISCUSSION STARTER:

As women, we are efficient in nurturing others, making sure things are done especially when it comes to our children or even our spouses. How do you feel when it looks like your hands are tied and things are out of your control?

I have an issue with time. I get frustrated when things take too long to get done or to be resolved. What are some your time issues?

What is your reaction when God has put something in your spirit to do and others are hindrances?

Notes:

WRITE YOUR OWN PRAYER OF BEING IN A NARROW PLACE

_____

_____

_____

_____

_____

_____

_____

_____

_____

_____

_____

_____

_____

_____

_____

_____

Waiting for an answer...

What did God say? Write it down.

Day 40 Create an Atmosphere

MUSIC: Bishop Clarence E. McClendon presents the Harvest Fire Mega Mass Choir; "Lord You Are Welcome in This Place" Shout Hallelujah Released 2000 Integrity

Treats: Coffee Cake, Spiced Herbal Tea sounds like a treat you would present to a special guest.

Welcome

Dear Lord,

I woke up this morning with this song in my spirit.

It says:

"Lord you are welcome in this place,
Lord you are welcome in this place
Lord you are welcome in this place
Have your way."[30]

"This place" refers to my life. Lord, You are welcome even in the secret places I have hidden from everybody else. I gladly open them up to You. I see myself straightening the cushions on the sofa, dusting the furniture and getting ready for You to arrive. I'm waiting for You to tear up the lease and purchase the property. I'm tired of trying to lead my own life. You have always been the source of my joy and strength.

Other verses of the song say, "move by Your spirit in this place, send Your anointing" and "heal and deliver in this place." I am so excited about what You are going to do in my life. What a release! I look forward to dropping these concerns that I don't have the answers to and resting in Your deliverance. Move by Your spirit Lord. Throw open the doors of the closets, my cupboards and clean out my attic.

I can't make it without Your help, your supernatural power. Send Your anointing in this place. Work issues out of me, ideas, beliefs and misconceptions that create problems. Send your anointing Lord. Find the hidden things I hid from myself.

Walking around with sore spots and raw spots so sensitive to the touch, so sensitive to wrong words or wrong looks is no fun. I need healing once and for all and I'll be whole. Heal and deliver. No hiding Lord. Whatever it takes, have Your way. Amen.

Dear Child,

"Look at me. I stand at the door. I knock. If you hear me call and open the door, I'll come right in and sit down to supper with you. Revelations 3; 20 (Message Bible)

The Lord will guide you continually, And satisfy your soul in drought, And strengthen your bones; You shall be like a watered garden, And like a spring of water, whose waters do not fail. Isaiah 58:11(NKJV)

DISCUSSION STARTER:

- Looking at your heart as a house, what room do you feel could be off limits to God?

- In your heart house, what ideas, thoughts, or issues would you store in the attic

- What areas do you keep wide open to the eyes and moving of the Spirit?

Notes:

WRITE YOUR OWN PRAYER OF WELCOME TO GOD

_____
_____
_____
_____
_____
_____
_____
_____
_____
_____
_____
_____
_____
_____
_____
_____
_____
_____
_____
_____
_____
_____
_____
_____

Waiting for an answer...

What did God say? Write it down.

YOU'VE MADE IT!

Now that you have completed your journey, this is just the beginning to a newer, fuller lifestyle of reaching out to women in building godly relationships of love. I'm sure the bonding process with your sisters has gotten under way. You have enjoyed each other's company and have become accustomed to not only talking together but praying together. You've found out a lot more about each other and have begun to know your hearts. I pray that God has been speaking to you concerning yourself and your friendships. Don't stop reaching out in love. I encourage you to continue the journey with other friends. Let it catch on and spread. Stronger relationships make stronger individuals and stronger individuals make stronger churches.

Whether you choose to use this group of friends or another group to hone into, it may be time to take your friendship to the next level. Become a GIG. The second level takes you deeper where you will find the gold of your relationship. What it took to begin is what it will take to continue.

Remember not every friendship is on the same level. Those who are meant to be connected to you in deep ways will rise to the top.

I pray that the Sister Tips and Discussion Starters in the book have provided opportunities to pull that small group of girlfriends around you. But if you still have questions, here are some answers that may help.

Q. What's a GiG?

A. Having a GIG (an acronym for Girlfriends Interceding for Girlfriends) is having a small group of girlfriends that love God and love you.

Q. How do you find them?

A. Wherever friends are made. Church, work, and social activities like birthday parties, anywhere you go.

Q. How do I get started?

A. Look around your life. Who are your girlfriends now? Invite them to discuss becoming a GIG and begin praying together for each other's needs. You already know some of their needs because you're friends. Prayer keeps the relationship healthy and creates a bond like nothing else.

Q. What if I really don't have any girlfriends?

A. You're the perfect person for GIGs. God wants to bless you with friendships that He will use to fulfill His good purpose in your life. But you have to do something. Proverbs says if you are to have friends you must first make yourself friendly.

Q. But I've been hurt and have made a decision to not have friends. How do I get past that?

A. As with anything thing else God asks us to do, it takes a bit of faith. Go slowly. Find ways to reach out to others in love, (e.g. giving a greeting card to someone you know needs a lift or offering to pay for a fast food breakfast.) Little things mean a lot. Don't look for anything back, not even a thank you or a smile; just give it like you're giving an offering to the Lord. God will begin to lead you to sisters who love God as you do and who are in His plan for your life. Remember the Bible says if you give, it shall be given to you. Give your friendship by faith, honest, wholehearted and good, and you'll receive friendships, honest, wholehearted and good.

Q. Then what?

A. As friendships develop, conversation will allow you to see into each other's lives. Begin meeting to pray for each other's needs.

Q. Is a GIG only a prayer group?

A. A GIG is built on prayer but it is a regular friendship that includes all the things we do as girlfriends, but better.

Building friendships takes Time, Risk, Opportunity and Talk. It's a slow T.R.O.T. but the rewards are worth every step! I must say this again, while we are commanded to love our sisters and brothers like we love ourselves, we are not commanded to become close intimate friends with everyone. So let God lead you. I believe by now you will know who God has put in your life for close communication.

God bless you!

APPENDIX

Here are some ideas to get you started when planning your six girlfriend outings. These fun-filled activities will give you and your friends space to discuss one or two of the topics you read from the Love Better; Live Happier guidebook. For example:

1. Have a movie night and use the theme of the movie to discuss something you want to discuss from the Love Better guidebook
2. Paint and Sip
3. Go bowling
4. Have a zoom night
5. Have a Karaoke night
6. Go to a fancy restaurant
7. Go to an Art show
8. Go to an amusement park
9. Try using a Groupon
10. Have your own photo shoot with your phone cameras

These are just some ideas. By all means create your own. But have fun! That's what's important.

ABOUT THE AUTHOR

Gwen Henry is an Pastor, wife of forty-eight years to date, a mother of five and a grandmother of an ever increasing number. She is the visionary and director of Sister Talk Ministries, a women's ministry that provided training, opportunities and outlets for women to form covenant relationships, helping them to walk together in harmony through the power of God's love. She presently lives with her husband in Atlanta, GA.

To contact Pastor Gwen Henry go to:
pastorgwen143@gmail.com Or www.pastorgwen.com

ENDNOTES

Chapter 2

1   Gibbs Lynn, "Every Real Housewives Series," screenrant, 8 June 2022, https://screenrant.com/real-housewives-series-ranked by ratings
2   Rick Warren, Purpose Driven Life (Grand Rapids, Mich.: Zondervan, 2002), 145-151
3   "TV Shoe Theme Songs – Cheers." Web Page. Apple to the Core Shopping and More. appletothecore.com/tvshowthemesongs/cheers
4   "The Names of G-D." Web Page. Judaism 101. jewfaq.org/name.htm

Chapter 3

5   Webster"s II New Riverside Dictionary, 1st edition, (New York: Houghton Mifflin Company, 1984), 370
6   Carrie Oliver and Erin Smalley, Grown-Up Girlfriends (Carol Stream, Illinois: Tyndale House Publishers, 2007), 41-46
7   "Health Risks of Loneliness Comparable to Smoking, Alcoholism and Obesity." Men's News Daily 29 Jul. 2010 mensnewsdaily.com/sexandmetro/2010/07/29/health-risks-of- loneliness-comparable-to-smoking-alcoholism-and-obesity
8   Tara Parker-Pope, " Well; What are Friends For? A Longer Life." New York Times 21 April, 2009. query.nytimes.com/gst/fullpage.html?res=9406EFD8103FF932A15757C0A96F9C8B63&scp=5&sq=april+21%2C+2009&st=nyt
9   ibid
10 Dr. Jackie Black, Ph.D., "The Difference Between Solitude and Loneliness," singlecafe.net/solitude.html

11 "Enjoli, The Perfume for Transition Feminist: An Add From the 70s {Perfume Images and Adverts}." Web page. Scented Salamander. mimifroufrou.com/ scentedsalamander/2009/10/enjoli_the_perfume_ for_transit.html

12 "Never Let Them See You Sweat." Web page. Dry Idea. dryidea.com

13 Dr. Jackie Black, Ph.D., "The Difference Between Solitude and Loneliness," singlecafe.net/solitude.html

Chapter 4

14 Harper Collins Bible Dictionary by Paul J. Achtemeier general editor with the society of Biblical literature, © 1985, 1996 Harper Collins Publishers 10 E. 53rd St NY. 10022 p618

15 Matthew Henry Commentary on the Whole Bible, Hendrickson Publishers ©1991, 2008 P.O. Box 3473 Peabody, Mass. 01961-3173, pp.351 chapter 4 verses 1-8

Chapter 5

16 Jackie Matthews, Factors Affecting "Fight or Flight" and "Tend or Befriend" Responses to Stress" Web page, University of Libriaries,Research Works Archives, 07/06/2005 digital.lib. washington.edu/researchworks/handle/1773/2071

17 Gary Smalley and John Trent, Love is a Decision (Nashville, Tenn. :Thomas Nelson Publishers, 1989), 41-52

18 Suzan Johnson, Becoming a Woman of Destiny (: New York, NY, Jeremy Tarcher/ Penguin, 2010), 181

19 John and Stasi Eldredge, Captivating (Nashville, Tenn.: Thomas Nelson Publishers, 2005), 25

Day 4

20 Greatest Hits Vol #1 by Randy Travis; released September 15, 1992; country; Warner Bros. Records; Producer Kyle Lehning; length:36:15

21 Stasi Etergde.....

22 Beth McHugh. "The Power of Friendship" Weblog entry. Health Mental Health. mental-health.families.com/blog/the-power-of-friendship

Day 6

23 Michelle McKinney Hammond, Sassy Single and Satisfied (Oregon: Harvest House Publisher, 2003), 173

Day 7

24 ibid

25 Day 23 - Joyce Meyers, Battlefield of the Mind (Oregon: Harvest House Publishers, 2001), 119-130

26 Day 26 - "The Cosby Show TV Series 1984-1992," Internet Movie Database, imb.com/title/tt0086687 (acquired November 3, 2010)

27 Day 29 - Bill and Pam Farrel: Red Hot Mahogany (Oregon: Harvest House Publishers)

28 Day 31 - Joyce Meyer, I Dare You (New York: Faith Words, 2007) pg. 113

29 Day 37 - Source unknown, "Never Alone," The New National Baptist Hymnal, arr. Eldon Burkwall, (Nashville, Triad Publications), p.127 1968 by Singspiration

30 Day 40 - Kurk Lykes, "Lord You are Welcome in this Place," Clarence McClendon and the Fire Harvest Mega Choir, (Shout Hallelujah, Released 2000 Integrity).

www.ingramcontent.com/pod-product-compliance
Lightning Source LLC
Chambersburg PA
CBHW061137120626
46546CB00005B/1831